Day of the Tentacle

Bob Mackey

Boss Fight Books
Los Angeles, CA
bossfightbooks.com

ISBN 13: 978-1-940535-33-3
First Printing: 2023

Series Editor: Gabe Durham
Associate Editor: Michael P. Williams
Book Design by Cory Schmitz

For Nina, who once dedicated a book to my parrot.

CONTENTS

FOREWORD BY LARRY AHERN

Tentacle Days – Time-traveling into Our Gaming Past

When Bob asked me to write the foreword to his *Day of the Tentacle* book, I was a bit surprised. I wasn't even a writer on the game; I did character design/animation (although I did go on to write several games since). Am I even qualified? Honestly, I wasn't sure I even knew what a foreword was, other than one of those sections we all skip to get to the actual book. Okay, maybe I am qualified.

Also, the project was so long ago that I've probably forgotten enough to fill several books, so really my only option was to just make up some stuff that hopefully approximates what it was like to work on this witty, irreverent, once-in-a-lifetime computer game (or so I've heard it described). Thankfully, Bob has done some painstaking research here conducting interviews with others who have much better memories (or are just better storytellers).

But if I remember correctly, we made the game back in the 90s when we all wore flannel and hung out with Kurt Cobain. There were only about 50 people in the entire division at the time, so the LucasArts art department was a pretty small group. Picture an 80s office building with lots of oak trim and fifteen heavy oak desks crammed in a small room. (I knew they were heavy because we constantly had to rearrange them for changing project teams.)

I was hired to make pixelated game characters, a process not unlike creating mosaics in ancient Greece. Thankfully, I had a better computer than the ancient Greeks to animate them with. I had just finished *Monkey Island 2: LeChuck's Revenge*, where I kept showing Ron Gilbert roughs of Guybrush slipping on banana peels and getting crushed by anvils in hopes of convincing him to include them in the game when the call went out to staff a sequel to *Maniac Mansion.* Luckily, Tim Schafer and Dave Grossman recognized my struggle and offered to give my slapstick inclinations a home.

We all bonded over a drive to do something forward-looking. So, naturally, we were inspired by looking back at the animated cartoon shorts of the 40s. Peter Chan had already done brilliant art on *LeChuck's Revenge,* so he was a natural to create the colorful, skewed environments of the new game. In college, I dabbled in animation but found the process to be quite tedious. Then the company offered to pay me to drop anvils on characters' heads and my opinion completely changed. I enthusiastically signed on to lead the animation effort. (Remember: 50 people in the whole company. I got lucky.)

I should probably come clean now and admit that I may have misremembered the whole hanging out with Kurt Cobain part. However, we did listen to his music, and the team did feel a bit like a band—one in its early days when that first album comes together easily because everyone's been jamming on the material awhile before laying it down on floppy disc. And, like any good first album, we didn't have the time or budget to get overly ambitious. Plus, it was a sequel to the already impressive *Maniac Mansion*. So, really, it was more like getting to make "Smells Like Teen Spirit 2."

Okay, I admit we really just wanted to be in a band instead of making nerdy computer games. (Well, in addition to making them. Maybe making them in secret? Game development back then was not the rockstar career it is today.) And, in fact, after we shipped, Tim, Dave, Kyle Balda, and I actually did start a band. It only lasted a few months (we lost our practice space), and then we had to make a choice between games and music. Recently I visited Seattle's Museum of Pop

Culture and discovered *Day of the Tentacle* on display right next to Kurt Cobain's guitar. Well, technically it's in the science fiction wing nowhere near the cool rock memorabilia. But it's still in the same building. So, I think we made the right choice.

THE STORY OF
ADVENTURE GAMES

To UNDERSTAND WHAT MAKES *Day of the Tentacle* so great—and book-worthy—you must first understand the adventure game. It's a genre that once carved out a very sustainable niche in the PC market, and eventually lost mindshare to games like *Doom*, which came to redefine the PC as a home to fast-paced action games. Another blow to adventure games came when so many of their unique qualities gradually found their way into other genres: voice acting, dialogue trees, a focus on storytelling and characterization, and other elements that had made them such boutique experiences.

After a brief period of hibernation in the 00s, Telltale Games revived and reinvented this type of experience with episodic revivals of adventure game classics, and, of course, an extremely critically and financially successful adaptation of *The Walking Dead* comic book series. While the original incarnation of Telltale Games went out of business—mostly due to company mismanagement rather than player disinterest—adventure games still quietly thrive in many different incarnations.

Though they articulate themselves in a variety of ways, all adventure games usually follow a similar approach. This genre features experiences that are typically slow-paced, with an emphasis on narrative over action. In an adventure game, the player progresses not by running, jumping, shooting, or stabbing—at least, not directly—but via vast networks of interconnected puzzles that rely on dialogue, inventory items, or both. In a pre–first-person-shooter era where action games often clumsily pushed against the limits of pre-Pentium hardware, adventures excelled as the types of games PCs did best.

That's roughly 40 years of adventure game history in a nutshell, but where did it all begin? The genre as we know it today has its roots in the age of computer games before graphics, only within the reach of the relatively few people who could access room-filling mainframe systems—most often on college campuses. Though they may be extremely primitive now, text-based games like *Hunt the Wumpus* and *Colossal Cave Adventure* offered a degree of narrative sophistication and complexity far greater than the *Pong* clones and simple Atari VCS games of the late 1970s. Even though text adventures persisted throughout the 80s and still exist today, graphics eventually became an expected feature of the adventure game, making the genre much more accessible and enticing than anything featuring a sterile screen of white-on-black text. And that's where Sierra On-Line comes in.

In 1980, Sierra (then known as On-Line Systems) released *Mystery House*, the first graphical adventure game. Though it still asked the player to input text for commands via the same means as graphics-free adventure games, its harsh, vector-based illustrations provided important context previously only left to the imagination. It didn't take long for Sierra to become the dominant force in the adventure game market, and throughout the 80s, the developer became synonymous with the genre thanks to the very effective branding of its various "quest" series of games: King's Quest, Space Quest, Police Quest, Quest for Glory, and the adult-themed Leisure Suit Larry—perhaps breaking the pattern because "Sex Quest" would have been too much for Reagan-era software stores.

Sierra developed an intense fan following despite (or perhaps because of) the fact that their games were adversarial and cruel to an absolutely comical level. They didn't set out to make frustrating and tedious experiences, though. It was simply the style at the time for adventure games to punish simple curiosity with death, lock players into fail states for seemingly arbitrary reasons, and turn every screen into a guessing game where players had to pin down the name of a crudely rendered object out of several possible synonyms. (Is that cluster of green leaves on the screen a bush? A shrub? A thicket?) Though these choices have made many Sierra adventures age particularly poorly, their games aren't bad—just designed for an entirely different audience with different expectations. Modern game designers now understand the perfect amount of friction to build into a video game to make it a satisfying experience; often, Sierra adventure games were *mostly* friction.

During the rise of Sierra On-Line, LucasArts (originally known as Lucasfilm Games) came into being. LucasArts started its life within Lucasfilm's computer division as the Games Group, and its initial releases have nothing to do with the developer's adventure games legacy. In the early- to mid-80s, LucasArts started off making zippy, technological showpieces that did an effective job of simulating 3D graphics on underpowered hardware: games like *Ballblazer*, *Rescue on Fractalus!*, and *Koronis Rift*. Even though George Lucas owned the company, thanks to an exclusivity deal with Atari, LucasArts could not make Star Wars games—an unfortunate stipulation when you consider the studio found itself housed within Skywalker Ranch, the private playground of Lucas himself. This would change at the dawn of the 90s, but until then, LucasArts would have to populate their games with new worlds and characters. Developer Ron Gilbert, who joined the company in 1985 and eventually spearheaded its adventure game efforts, didn't enter the LucasArts fold as a fan of the genre—in fact, his experience was limited to dabbling with the text-based mainframe game *Adventure* at his local college.

When it came time for Gilbert and his LucasArts collaborator, Gary Winnick, to develop *Maniac Mansion*, the two had a visual concept in mind, but absolutely no genre. Their homage to classic B-movies mixed with a wink at the then-burgeoning slasher genre had a cast of characters and a setting, but the two couldn't think of a basic gameplay concept to power these creative ideas. It wasn't until Gilbert saw a graphical adventure game for the first time that he realized the shape *Maniac Mansion* needed to take: "I went down to see my aunt for Christmas, and my cousin was playing [the original] *King's Quest*, and that was the first time I had seen any of the King's Quest games and the first time I had ever seen an adventure game with graphics," Gilbert told me in a 2015 interview for USgamer. "My understanding of adventure games before that were all text, and I just watched him play, and it was like this epiphany moment... Like 'Oh, this is what *Maniac Mansion* needs to be. It needs to be an adventure game with these pictures on it.'"

This "adventure game with pictures on it" was released for the PC in 1987 as *Maniac Mansion*, a modest hit that reinvented adventure games from a much-needed outsider's perspective. And thanks to Gilbert and Winnick being new to the genre and not knowing the perceived limitations, *Maniac Mansion*'s design ended up being remarkably ambitious, even when compared to much later games in the LucasArts catalog. In his mission to rescue his girlfriend Sandy from the demented Dr. Fred Edison's brain-sucking Zom-B-Matic machine, protagonist Dave can recruit two of six friends, each with different abilities that lead to different puzzle chains and endings. To complicate things further, players must coordinate the actions, inventories, and locations of all three characters to finish the game, all while the residents of the titular mansion go about their normal routines—often via then-novel "cutscenes," which cut away from the playable characters' perspectives.

Thanks to its very user-friendly nature, *Maniac Mansion* remains incredibly approachable, and was undoubtedly a huge breath of fresh air to adventure gamers of the late 80s. The game drops the then-standard text interface in favor of a "point and click" system that tasks players with building command sentences by clicking on a list of verbs at the bottom of the screen along with the actual objects in the Mansion's many rooms—no more guesswork involved! Outside of a few minor instances, the chance to paint yourself into a fail-state corner proved shockingly rare. And character deaths either amounted to Easter eggs players had to work fairly hard to see, or very obvious fatal scenarios (like pushing an ominous red button at the bottom of a drained swimming pool). Failing was much more challenging than, say, neglecting to pick up an innocuous item early in the game, only to have that be your undoing a dozen hours later. Gilbert and his LucasArts peers would later refine their craft even further a few years down the road by sanding down the rough edges of *Maniac Mansion*'s design sense, but this 1987 release marked the beginning of the developer's "house style"— one echoed in modern adventure games more than 30 years later.

Essential to the development of *Maniac Mansion* is the foundation the game rests on, aptly called SCUMM: Script Creation Utility for Maniac Mansion. To put it simply, this game engine—developed by Gilbert and LucasArts programmer Chip Morningstar—allowed *Maniac Mansion* to be designed and tested using a simple scripting language that could be learned and implemented fairly quickly by programming novices. In terms of how SCUMM influenced design, thanks to its ease of use, it allowed developers to quickly proto-type new ideas, which led to more refined puzzles and a somewhat improvisational style of game development. It saw many improvements over the next decade or so, but SCUMM remained the foundation of LucasArts adventure games until the GrimE engine came along in 1998. This engine, developed for and named after their 1998 adventure game *Grim Fandango*, replaced SCUMM's 2D sprites with 3D polygons set against pre-rendered backgrounds.

Though Sierra would forever dominate LucasArts in the sales department, after its success on the Commodore 64 and other platforms, *Maniac Mansion* had quite a bit of staying power. Within just a handful of years, this modest adventure game saw a very good 1990 port for the Nintendo Entertainment System, a three-season Canadian sitcom adaptation that featured some glaring—and questionable—differences from the source material, and the 1993 sequel this book is devoted to. Though LucasArts had dabbled in adventure games a year before *Maniac Mansion* with an adaptation of the David Bowie movie, *Labyrinth*, Ron Gilbert's off-kilter adventure about tentacles, teens, and trouble sparked an internal interest in the genre that would continue at the developer for years to come.

After a few years and a few other adventure games like *Indiana Jones and the Last Crusade* and *Zak McKraken and the Alien Mindbenders*, 1990's *The Secret of Monkey Island* kicked off the studio's most prolific adventure game series with four entries and two remakes before its transition from video game developer to licensing brand for Disney. Also directed by Ron Gilbert, *The Secret of Monkey Island* was developed alongside the writing of his manifesto, "Why Adventure Games Suck and What We Can Do About It." Published in December of 1989 in the *Journal of Computer Game Design*, this document takes the lessons Ron learned from the making of *Maniac Mansion* and takes a hardline stance in favor of user-friendliness.

"Puzzles and their solutions need to make sense," begins one of Gilbert's Rules of Thumb. "They don't have to be obvious, just make sense. The best reaction after solving a tough puzzle should be, 'Of course, why didn't I think of that sooner!' The worst, and most often heard after being told the solution is, 'I never would have gotten that!' If the solution can only be reached by trial and error or plain luck, it's a bad puzzle."

To modern ears, Gilbert's late-80s cry for fairness in game design may not feel all that revolutionary. But that's because so much of the wisdom in his highly informed rant has been codified by the games industry. And while Gilbert meant for his advice to pertain specifically to the adventure game format, you can easily apply the insight from his manifesto to many other genres. When you look at the kind of player abuse that was permissible at the beginning of the 90s, it's clear that Gilbert was seeing where the future needed to go to keep players from ragequitting adventure games for good.

And these rules led to *The Secret of Monkey Island* being perhaps the most celebrated entry in the LucasArts adventure game library. Though this first *Monkey Island* still contains a few dated adventure game elements—like game-padding mazes—it contains no dead ends, no fail states, and only a single way for the player to die—and a very clever one at that. At a certain point in the game, protagonist Guybrush Threepwood ends up in an underwater death trap with a heavy idol anchoring him to the sea floor. The solution is deceptively simple—pick up the idol and walk out of your would-be briny grave—but *Monkey Island* taunts the player by putting several rope-severing items just out of reach.

With so few possible interactions in this scene, it's nearly impossible not to stumble upon the solution eventually. But you can always stick around and test Guybrush's claim that he can hold his breath for ten minutes. If you do, Guybrush dies, and the game keeps going. Once dead, the verbs you normally use to interact with the world all become actions more associated with a water-logged corpse (like "float" and "bloat").

In the Ron Gilbert school of game design, death isn't around every corner; rather, it's an Easter egg.

The Secret of Monkey Island is also notable in that it features the first LucasArts design work of Tim Schafer and Dave Grossman, future directors of *Day of the Tentacle*. Schafer and Grossman, both hired in September of 1989, ended up providing over two-thirds of the writing for *The Secret of Monkey Island*. When they started writing, Schafer assumed that they were just creating placeholder dialogue that Ron would later replace with more professional-sounding text, which is probably what gives some of the jokes have such a casual and off-the-cuff air.

After working with Schafer and Grossman once again to create 1991's *Monkey Island 2: LeChuck's Revenge*, Gilbert departed LucasArts to form Humongous Entertainment, makers of adventure game series for the younger set (Putt-Putt, Pajama Sam, Freddi Fish) now fondly remembered by aging millennials. With the absence of their former mentor, Dave and Tim found themselves in the shared director's chair for the first time, and at the helm of a sequel to the game that made LucasArts a contender in the adventure game genre.

1993's *Day of the Tentacle* doesn't completely rely on the first game for context, but the plot provides a compelling hook, whether you've played *Maniac Mansion* or not, and sets up this sequel's excellent time-travel premise. After the nefarious Purple Tentacle intentionally swallows toxic waste and grows two stubby little arms, he goes on a world-conquering spree, leaving *Maniac Mansion*'s Bernard—and two of his college friends—to save the human race by jumping back to yesterday to turn off the machine pumping the deadly catalyst into the water supply. Unfortunately, a time-travel mishap lands the rotund roadie Hoagie 200 years in the past, and the unhinged med student Laverne 200 years into the tentacle-dominated future, leaving the three heroes with no choice but to figure out how to jump back to the present (and then back to yesterday) to prevent this global horror from unfolding. Like any good LucasArts adventure, *Day of the Tentacle*'s central idea is delightfully (and uniquely) convoluted.

So where do I factor into all of this? To tell the truth, I approach this *Day of The Tentacle* book project from a former place of envy. When I was growing up, my lower-middle class family didn't have the means to start owning the once-obligatory home PC until late 1996, meaning I didn't get to experience the joy of adventure games until the final years of their first phase. I had my first taste of the genre with the NES port of *Maniac Mansion* and wanted more, but there wasn't more to be had on my console. I would pore over the PC game boxes at my local Software Etc., buy issues of *PC Gamer* with enclosed demo diskettes I couldn't use, and dream

When I first entered the games press full-time in 2011, I made it my self-indulgent goal to talk to everyone still living who made my favorite games, so it shouldn't come as a surprise that I had *Day of the Tentacle* directors Dave Grossman and Tim Schafer on my podcast, *Retronauts*. That was an intensely gratifying experience, but it put the wheels in motion for something much larger and more in-depth—a full oral history of a game that was far from overlooked, but not explored nearly as much as its contemporaries. Thankfully, the announcement of Double Fine's *Day of the Tentacle Remastered* gave me the chance to speak with most of the relatively small crew behind the game, and after hours and hours of interviews, writing, and editing, I'd published a three-part oral history of the game for the website, USgamer.

What you're about to read consists of most of that original oral history, but greatly expanded, tweaked, and given additional context since its original 2016 publishing. Even with the privilege of putting together a project like this, things move fast on the internet, and time can be frustratingly limited. So when I thought of pitching a project to Boss Fight Books, one of the first ideas I landed on involved expanding those three articles into a comprehensive work. And thanks to the permission of USgamer and the deadline-extending generosity of Boss Fight Books, you're finally holding it in your hands. It's extremely fulfilling for me, and as a bonus I finally have something to give my mom, who always tells me, "You should write a book!" (She never said the book had to be about a subject she remotely understands.)

With all that said, I hope you enjoy this comprehensive exploration of a very special game from a very special era. All the developers of *Day of the Tentacle* have gone on to do some pretty wonderful things, but there's a "lightning in a bottle" quality to the project that really represents the second generation of LucasArts talent forging an exciting new path ahead for the developer's remaining years of adventure game development. So read on, and remember what they say: If you want to save the world, you gotta push a few old ladies down the stairs.

DAY OF THE TENTACLE

adventure," and somehow conveyed the bold poses, squash-and-stretch action, and stylized backgrounds of classic animation while trapped under the constraints of a 320 x 200 resolution.

Day of the Tentacle is more than just an artistic achievement, though. Its time-travel premise tasks players with exploring three different versions of the titular *Maniac Mansion*—past, present, and future—using straightforward cause-and-effect logic to make its puzzles more reasonable (not to mention ingenious). All these qualities, combined with *DotT*'s memorable and unique cast of characters, make this unassuming little sequel one of the greatest adventure games of all time.

Much like the original *Maniac Mansion*, *Day of the Tentacle* allows you to switch between its three different characters on the fly—but this time around, they're affixed to their own time periods. Essentially, you're exploring three different eras of the Edison Mansion: A run-down hotel hosting a novelty goods convention in the present, a Constitution-writing retreat in the past, and a home full of hostile tentacles in the future. While many of the puzzles never stray from their respective time periods, the more rewarding ones play off the cause-and-effect relationships of our own reality: Age some cheap wine for 400 years, for instance, and you'll have a fine bottle of fresh vinegar. And if for some reason you need to shrink a sweater down to hamster-size, simply stick it in a dryer and pump enough quarters in there to make it run for decades. From the outset, *Day of the Tentacle* does an excellent job of communicating the central goal for each character—wrapping your brain around the puzzle chains that lead to said goals, however, is another story altogether.

While *Day of the Tentacle*'s puzzles excel by allowing you to apply your knowledge of temporal rules to its consistently zany internal logic, the characters and writing help sell the experience as the interactive cartoon LucasArts set out to make. Each of the playable characters may be a total misfit, but the careful work of directors Tim Schafer and Dave Grossman make them endearing rather than grating—especially Bernard, who makes for a more meek and socially awkward nerd than the shrill and often creepy Urkels and Screeches of the 90s. It also helps that no character in the game is truly "normal"—even the Founding Fathers find themselves reduced to cowards, idiots, and self-important blowhards. (Which feels more risqué than intended in our modern age of founding father deifying uber-patriotism.) When you're bashing your head against a puzzle, just watching these characters bounce off each other can provide an all-important release valve to dissipate some frustration.

Indeed, *Day of the Tentacle* was made for a much different world—one not beset with smartphones, fast internet access, and enough free and/or practically free entertainment to last several lifetimes. While most modern games simply won't allow the player to get lost for more than a few minutes (if that), games like *DotT* always required a bit of downtime from the player: time to walk away from the game, only to have an "a-ha!" moment while taking a shower or doing something similarly mundane.

Even though I internalized *DotT*'s puzzle solutions years ago, compared to the rest of the LucasArts library, it feels the most fair—or, at the very least, the least likely to leave you absolutely stumped. In a very smart move, Schafer and Grossman gradually expand just how much of *DotT*'s world can be explored, if only to avoid overwhelming the player: The experience opens with just Bernard and Hoagie available, limiting the number of viable puzzles in progress. Once you manage to free Laverne and can access the future, you should be more than prepared to juggle a handful of objectives at once.

DESIGN

Origins

After the release of 1991's Monkey Island 2: LeChuck's Revenge, *designers Tim Schafer and Dave Grossman found themselves in the position of project leaders following the departure of Ron Gilbert. The only question left for them: "What, exactly, do we do now?"*

Tim Schafer: Ron [Gilbert], who was our project manager on *Monkey Island*, thought we were ready to be project leaders, and he told management, "I think Tim and Dave should be project leaders." And, they were like, "What should we have them do?" And, Dave and I—I think we were too scared to actually come up with something new at the time. And they were like, "You want to do a sequel to *Maniac Mansion*?" We were like, "Yes, yes." That was a big relief, that we didn't have to come up with a whole new game our first time out.

Dave Grossman: There were some ideas already floating around, and Ron had said he had always wanted to do a time travel game. I think there were a few other proposals, actually, besides that. I wouldn't swear to it, because I remember settling on the time travel thing pretty quickly. We all liked that a lot.

Luckily, the team was also equipped with a game engine that was created for Maniac Mansion and had been used for every LucasArts adventure since.

Oliver Franzke, Lead Programmer of *DotT Remastered*, in his GDC 2017 talk: *Day of the Tentacle* was created with an engine called SCUMM, which stands for Script Creation Utility for Maniac Mansion. It was developed in the mid- to late-80s at LucasArts for the cult classic adventure game *Maniac Mansion*. It was a revolutionary piece of technology and powered a lot of great games. [These include *The Dig*, *Full Throttle*, and all three Monkey Island games.]

Ron Gilbert in his GDC 2011 *Maniac Mansion* Postmortem: After a few weeks of frantic programming, it became clear to me that I was never going to complete *MM* writing the whole thing in 6502 assembly language. Another programmer at Lucasfilm by the name of Chip Morningstar suggested that I create a scripting language. This would allow the logic of the game to be done in scripting language and the engine itself could be done in blazingly fast 6502. Chip wrote that first version of the SCUMM compiler and I wrote the interpreter, and the rest of the engine, and the SCUMM system was born.

Oliver Franzke, GDC 2017: As a programmer, the first question I ask myself is, "What made SCUMM so special?" What we figured out quickly was that SCUMM was the first major reusable game engine. In the mid- to late-80s it was common to write your entire game, including the gameplay in C or even Assembly. With SCUMM, the developers went in a completely different direction by moving all the gameplay logic into a high-level domain-specific language. The SCUMM engine introduced scripting or at least popularized scripting in the games industry.

Schafer and Grossman got some good ideas out of Gilbert before his departure.

TS: Ron was actually around for the beginning of the design process, and then he left to start Humongous [Entertainment], and Dave and I were on our own to really run with it. [We] brought on Larry Ahern and Peter Chan to do the art, and that's when we really gelled as a team and took off. But yeah, the whole idea of time travel was Ron's.

TS: [Ron and Dave] came up with that idea, and then Ron says, "That sounds like a good idea. Here's a document that Gary and I already wrote." And it was a two pager, I think, two to five pages, of the basic premise of the time travel thing, and the sludge and the tentacles being behind it.

DG: There wasn't any detail beyond that. There was no, "Let's go to this time period or that time period." That was something that the four of us all sat down and worked out together. So, it was Tim and I, [and] Ron and Gary [Winnick] all sitting in a room. The way we did that was mostly to think about different time periods and what would be the kinds of things that we would be able to do there, who we might meet and talk to, and to some degree, some puzzles that might work. But we didn't really think about it too much at that stage. And, a few prospects had a lot of meat to them, and some others didn't. "Oh, this Revolutionary War period has a lot of stuff that sings for all of us," and so we wanted to include that one. And we felt like, the future, we've got to do that, so, there's nothing specific about it, but it allows us to philosophize about some cause and effect and societies and stuff like that. So, that seemed cool.

TS: When we first pitched [*DotT*], everyone at the review meeting was like, "There's too many characters.

You have 35, you could cut it down to 30." And so, what we mostly did was, we didn't cut anybody, we combined characters. So, we had the cold guy, and I think we made him John Hancock... we had Thomas Jefferson and the log guy. [So we made] them the same character. That way we could say we cut a character, but really we just put them together, and that probably was better for editing anyway.

DG: We always felt like, canon is canon, so we should treat the events of the first game as real in every respect and follow on them, but, in terms of doing the game that felt the same way, or even following the style, we were explicitly told that we didn't have to do that. And the reason for that was that a good five years or so had gone by, and so, computers were just capable of different stuff, and a lot of stuff just felt different. And it just felt like, if we tried to hew to the style, it would be too retro. So, it was Kelly Flock [who] was running the game's division at that time, and he just basically said, not, "Go crazy," but, "Make something good rather than making something that's exactly like *Maniac Mansion*."

TS: We actually had six [playable] characters in the original [concept], and our original intention was to use all of them. Well, you know, the original *Maniac* had six or seven, so, we were going to let you pick three from that in the same way that that game did. When we started calculating the workload of making the game before we even designed the first room of it, that immediately seemed like it was just going to balloon things well out of proportion for what we would actually do, because now we were having to support a lot more specific animations and stuff.

TS: [Bernard and Razor are] the strongest high-concept characters [from *Maniac Mansion*], just being a punk and a nerd. A lot of the other ones... like Mike. What's his name? No, Dave. Just the fact that I can't remember his name [proves he's unremarkable].

DG: Bernard—we just felt very enamored of him, always, from day one. He was everybody's favorite character from the first game, so he was kind of a given. He was kind of the nerdy one, so having the cool dumb one and the crazy one, that felt like a good counterpoint to us. And then, the other characters, I remember, there was Moonglow, who was this hippie girl who ended up on the cutting room floor. There was Chester, who was this tall skinny artist who wound up being remade into Ned and Jed Edison. So, we just took the character design for him and used him for them instead, saved ourselves a little extra work.

TS: We found a document that has the six kids, and it was Bernard, Hoagie, Laverne, Chester, Moonglow, and Razor. So we picked the two that were our favorites, Razor and Bernard, and then added these four. And then, at our first pitch meeting, everyone's like, "There's too many characters in this game. You're never going to get it done on time. Cut half the characters." And so I cut it down to three.

Still, eventually every MM *character made it into* DotT, *if not in the way you'd expect.*

Oliver Franzke, GDC 2017: As rumor has it, when the original team was working on *DotT*, Ron Gilbert came by one day and noticed that one environment in *DotT* is actually as big as the entire game of *Maniac Mansion*. And so he continued, "Wouldn't it be funny if you could just play *Maniac Mansion* within *DotT*?" So this feature was added.

•

A Tag Team of Directors

While Ron Gilbert once acted as their supervisor, Schafer and Grossman now found themselves taking on his singular role. But this shared position didn't lead to a battle of egos—in fact, the credits of Day of the Tentacle *are programmed to randomly list either Schafer or Grossman's name first—leaving the matter of "top billing" to a random*

*number generator. This kind of egalitarian company cul-
ture led to a very collaborative production process, where
artists, animations, writers, designers, and programmers
were free to contribute their own ideas.*

TS on the podcast Dev Game Club (DGC) in 2016:
[Grossman and I both] started [at LucasArts] on the
same day in September of '89.

TS: I always really valued working with Dave, because
we worked together and shared an office for years, and
we never had a conflict about anything. I think we were
both very conflict-avoidy type people, and Dave was
just super mellow and very logical, talks things out. I
don't think we ever had a disagreement. If we would, it
was always just a friendly discussion. And we also [each]
had our areas of the game, maybe characters or dia-
logues we kind of owned. Just like [while we were working on] *Monkey Island*: I would do Stan the ship sales-
man, and Dave would do Herman Toothrot, and we
didn't tell each other how to do each other's characters.

*Ron Gilbert had already set the tone for an open-minded
and collaborative workplace.*

DG: If you had ideas, they would be heard. And the
team was [small enough] that you could just walk into
Ron's office and say, "Hey, I had a great idea for this part
of the game. What if... *ya ya ya ya ya*." And he would

always be super receptive to whatever you wanted to tell him, and he would know, pretty much right away [say], "That is a genius idea, let's put it in the game," or, "I don't think that quite works, and here's why." And he would always tell you why.

DG: The nature of collaboration didn't change at all. That wasn't a company change, just Tim and I got promoted, and we were now doing Ron's job. I at least took a lot of cues from Ron about how to do that job, because a lot of the way that the collaboration worked on his projects was a way I wanted collaboration to work. Super open, and there was a group of us whose job it was to sort of come up with the story and design the puzzles more or less at the same time, and we would do a lot of brainstorming on that. But other people were always welcome to come and be part of that process, or weigh in on whatever they felt like they needed to weigh in on.

TS: I often have referred to it as the Last Easy Project to Make, because there was no voice [acting] until the end and there was no 3D. So, everything was "what you see is what you get." We'd write text, it would be on the screen, they'd draw the art and put it on the screen. Everything was so smooth. And they had a very senior team, it was a very flat team, because we were always working for Ron. So, it's kind of like Ron left, and we were all on the same level. So, even though we were in charge and the artists worked for us, we were used to working side-by-side on *Monkey 2*.

TS in a 2012 interview with Rock, Paper, Shotgun: 3D and voices adds a lot of pressure on development. 3D takes so much longer to make all your characters. And voice definitely made it so you had to have things locked down early in production. You had to have the voices recorded, so you could start animating the cutscenes, which took a long time. But you don't have the dialogue written, because you want to playtest the game, see if you need to add dialogue, and it's this big complicated knot of dependencies. Voice always enhances a game, but on *DotT* we definitely did not have to worry about any of those things until the end. I don't know if that was the secret, or if it was just smaller production, or times were easier back then, but... it didn't have any crunch mode.

Schafer and Grossman also instituted new practices to help the project move smoothly, like the use of storyboarding.

TS: [*DotT*] was the first game where we storyboarded every single location beforehand. A lot of the times, on *Monkey Island*, it would be, you would just go, "What are we doing this week?" And Ron would be like, "Well, Steve [Purcell] just painted this room, why don't you wire it up." I think in his mind, he had it all mapped out, but, most of us were just taking the work as it came, and wiring it up, and working on it until it was time to stop. And this time, we actually made storyboards for every single location. [...] I think when you do a lot of that preplanning, it actually gives you more room to be improvisational, because you know what the scope is, you know what the boundaries are, you know how much room you have. So, it allows you to goof around a lot more, within that box that you've defined by planning it.

DG: In terms of Tim and I together, we had a good dynamic. It's almost like we were in a good marriage or something. I look for the same things in romantic partners as creative partners, and that's basically, "Does the synergy work well?" Like, when you're playing off each other, [the] ideas getting generated. And then, more importantly, how well you resolve differences. And for us, if we had two different opinions about something, we would talk about it for a couple minutes. And it would usually become apparent really quickly either who was right or who cared about it more. And, if it was the second thing, we generally would go with that. Someone would have more passion or feeling about it, so we'd just do it that way.

The team didn't know how good they had it.

DG: [Tim and I] were pretty harmonious. In retrospect, now, having been in the business for more than 25 years, you don't see that a lot, so I was actually kind of lucky to be partnered up with him for mostly the first five years of my career.

•

Stars and Slime Forever

Day of the Tentacle*'s use of a vital moment of American history—the writing of The Constitution—made for an inspired choice, and allowed figures like John Hancock, George Washington, Thomas Jefferson, and Ben Franklin to be drawn into the story of three college co-eds trying to stop an evil tentacle from taking over the world. Relying on such a specific chunk of Americana wasn't without its problems, though...*

TS: Going back to the formation of the country was just something that led to a lot of great puzzles. We could change the Constitution to include things that would help you solve puzzles, and it just naturally seemed really funny to us.

DG: You'll notice it's not real American history, but sort of legendary American history. Everybody is sort of fifth-grade interpretations of the things [we've] heard, so you get George Washington's cherry tree and the wooden teeth. So, when we were talking about American history, those things were all coming up, and I think the specific moment that we chose within that came out of a desire to literally change the country in a frivolous way by editing the Constitution. That was an idea that occurred to us. "Oh, yeah, if they're making the Constitution, then we can put stuff in it, and it will be silly and arbitrary and that'll be great." So, that was why [we decided on] exact dates for [the past], just so we could muck around with the Constitution.

TS: It's kind of a spoof of taking the bigger, more comical stereotypes about George Washington and the cherry tree. Then again, if you don't know the story about George and the cherry tree, that might be a weird puzzle to [solve]. But then, they're solved the way all adventure game puzzles are solved, which is just: You talk to all the characters and try all the objects, and eventually something gives you a hint.

With all the US history in the game, some at LucasArts were concerned with DotT's *reception overseas.*

DG: We figured we were doing things that were sort of so basic that they would be universal, and we weren't right about that. But that was what we thought, and we just went for it. I guess by that time, we knew already that basically a third of our audience was in Germany, so we probably should have thought more about that.

TS: Specifically, marketing and management were like, "You guys, no one knows who Ben Franklin is outside this country. This is not going to sell, but let's try it." And they told us it sold better in France than in America. Sold more in Germany than in America. And, the fact is, in Europe they're just better educated about American history than we are about European history.

DG: It doesn't, in retrospect, seem to have hurt [sales] very much. The game is still a success, and people are still talking about it. So I feel like we must have done something good. But if I had it to do over again, we might think a little bit more globally about it.

•

Thinking Like a Player

TS: You see in modern reviews of adventure games when they talk about how hard the puzzles are, I feel like those people did not poke on them enough. In the old days, you were expected to talk to everybody. Talk to everybody, exhaust the dialogue trees, try all the objects. If you're trying to open a door, and one of them will be like, "No, I can't use that, because it's rusted shut. If only I could break the rust," or something. Get some hint, "Oh, I think I know what to do now."

[...] A lot of time when playing adventure games, you wouldn't be able to solve a puzzle until you stopped playing, took a nap, went for a walk, or took a shower. And then you'd figure it out when you were walking around the corner, "Ah, I got it." Or, you'd just sit down and play it and you'd instantly get it, after struggling for an entire day the day before. And it's just that thing when you learn, even when you're not thinking about something you're thinking about it in your brain. It's like, *click click click click click*.

[...] The biggest change we made in playtesting [was] that originally in the game you could have access to all three kids at once, from the very beginning of the game. And we playtested that, and people were so confused. They didn't know where to go. They were kind of overwhelmed. So, we made that change where you could only play as Hoagie, and then you unlocked Bernard, and then you unlocked Laverne. That helped a lot.

Schafer and Grossman chalk up the game's open-endedness to their inexperience as lead developers.

DG on DGC Podcast: We were usually working with some variant of a three-act structure. The thing about *DotT* is that almost all of it is the middle. The first act is mostly the seven minutes of cutscene. And then they get sent through time, and then almost the whole game is them messing around in time. And then there's the tiny little end part. It's one gigantic miasma of puzzles. That makes it harder because you've got more stuff to think about, and there's a certain tension that develops in your brain when you have too much to think about. People get tense playing *DotT*.

TS on DGC Podcast: Nonlinearity is a word that we used as a general good thing. We had a lot of fun with—and people seemed to react well to—the three trials [to become a pirate] in [*The Secret of*] *Monkey Island*. We were always trying to make things nonlinear because adventure games can feel really scripted, like there's only one thing to do and you're just trying to guess what the designer wants you to do next, and if you can make it nonlinear then at least the player feels like they have some sort of agency. They're making some choice, like, "I'm gonna work on this section." It's like unraveling a knot: You don't just pull it off in one place—you don't just grab one strand and yank it. You pull this little part, and this little part, and that loosens up this other part. *DotT* is just one big knot.

Schafer and Grossman had their former boss's game design tenets in their heads while making the game.

DAY OF THE TENTACLE

TS on DGC Podcast: Ron had a lot of things that he believed really strongly from the beginning. He wrote this whole article about why adventure games suck and what we can do about it; that was right when Dave and I got hired, when he was grumpy about adventure games. His biggest pet peeve besides dying in games was backwards puzzles: He hated when you'd find a key and then find a locked door later and be like, "Oh, I have the key already."

DG on DGC Podcast: Rules came out organically when Ron asked questions about the puzzles. An important one I remember getting asked a lot was, "How's the player supposed to figure this out?" That has stuck with me. We always went to great lengths to make sure all the information was in there—we would have these big pizza orgies and [play]test everything. One of the things we were always looking for the most was: Are people getting stuck? And why?

One particularly tricky puzzle in DotT *involves swapping the locations of a squeaky mattress and a non-squeaky mattress in the same room so Hoagie can lure a cat far away enough to steal its mouse toy. This requires the player to use two non-inventory objects on each other, which is a fairly unusual interaction for a SCUMM game.*

DG on DGC Podcast: Some [puzzles] we would reject just because it was hard to do with the interface. Maybe we should have kicked that [mattress puzzle] out or redesigned it because what it turned into was what we call an "interface puzzle": The hardest thing about the puzzle is how you get the interface to do what you intend it to do. Easy to figure out and hard to make happen. And that's never fun.

•

Cause and Effect

More than any other LucasArts adventure, Day of the Tentacle *bucks the well-deserved bad reputation of its chosen genre and gives players plenty of tough-but-fair puzzles along with a variety of paths to explore whenever a dead-end rears its ugly head.*

While LucasArts' games always operated on their own off-kilter—but consistent—internal logic, Day of the Tentacle's *use of time travel allowed players to also apply their own knowledge of cause-and-effect space-time continuum relationships popularized by movies like* Back to the Future. *Looking back on their work, Schafer and Grossman still have their favorite puzzles—and both agree that a specific one didn't come out as well as intended.*

The puzzle in question tasks players with finding and charging a super-battery: Hoagie's main goal in the past. Once Hoagie has the battery in his possession, he can charge it by sneaking the device into Ben Franklin's famous kite experiment—but lightning won't strike unless Hoagie washes a nearby carriage first. Unfortunately, the suburban myth of how it tends to rain if you wash your car was lost on many players.

DG: [*DotT* isn't perfect], but I wouldn't change it. I think that I have taken a tack over the years of just, do the best you can in the moment that you're doing it, and then move on to the next thing. I wrote a poetry blog for 19 years. It was a weekly thing. And the whole thing was just an exercise in: Have a deadline that's this week, work on something, and then just stop and move on to the next thing—because it can be really hard as a writer to know when to stop. It's the same thing with these games. I look at *Day of the Tentacle*, and I look at that puzzle about washing the car to make it rain, and that's a thing that, at my house growing up, that was a known piece of lore. Everyone understood that whenever you washed your car, it would automatically make it rain.

TS: It was one of the [puzzles] that seemed a lot funnier at the time. Because of that, we thought that was a common expression, "How come every time I wash my car it rains?" It's not as bad as the monkey wrench puzzle in *Monkey Island 2*.

This puzzle involves using a monkey-wrench-shaped monkey to activate a pump—a needlessly obtuse puzzle in an otherwise elegantly designed game. When viewed in your inventory, the graphical representation of this monkey doesn't immediately resemble a monkey wrench, and, to make matters worse, this pun only works in American English. The German localization attempts to remedy this by giving a helpful hint when the player examines said monkey: "He is so stiff you could loosen a screw with him."

TS: I don't know how we expected anyone to get the monkey wrench one. But, the car wash one, as we were playing through it, we noticed a lot more hints. Like, if you try to do stuff with the car, [the game] talks about how dirty it is, and it talks about how, "Oh, I hate to wash it because every time I wash it, it rains." He has a hint in there.

DG: Yeah, [it's the car wash puzzle], I think, from that game, that I feel the worst about. In *Monkey 2*, it's the one with the monkey wrench, and the lesson there was, in large part, don't ever base a puzzle on a pun, because it won't work when you translate it to other languages. And not even that, it doesn't even work cross-culturally, because if you go to England, they don't call it a monkey wrench at all. It's a very American thing.

TS: You definitely can't help but see all the mistakes when you look back at an old game, but if enough time passes, you also tend to get this acceptance—it is what it is, and that's what it was—and I wouldn't want to go back and change much. [...] And it's funny, though. With other games, [definitely with] *Full Throttle*, [we'd] have to figure out something to do about that kicking-the-wall puzzle, and *Grim Fandango* had that signpost puzzle. There's always this one puzzle in every adventure game that I know everyone quits on. Whenever they say they don't finish [the game], I can usually guess where they stopped.

DG: I think the moments when [*DotT*] shines—and I probably would give you a different answer tomorrow—but I like the part about painting the stripe on the cat to turn it into a skunk, because that to me is an example of the game making you think like a cartoon character in order to succeed. So, that's a moment where you're feeling the most in tune with the material when you solved that puzzle. Now, the fact that you had to do it in this arbitrary way with the fence, and getting the paint on the fence first, I'm not as happy with that segment of the puzzle. But I like the end goal and idea of the puzzle more than the execution of it.

This puzzle involves finding a way to paint a white stripe down an innocuous cat—basically the premise of many

Pepe Le Pew cartoons—in order to scare the captive Edison family of the future out of their prison cell.

TS: I love the puzzles where you're changing America, because one of the things I like about adventure game puzzles is, when you finish it, and you're telling someone else the story of what you did in the game, that should be an entertaining story. And just telling someone that you changed the Constitution of America so that you can solve a puzzle in an adventure game, I feel like that's entertaining in and of itself.

DG: I love changing the flag, and I loved changing the Constitution. Again, it's not so much the puzzle [itself] as the very adventure game-y thing of mucking up something large in order to achieve some small personal goal. Adventure games seem to have a lot of that. You're always stealing things from people and ruining their lives, and you get the cook fired and you do this and you do that, and, "No, I just wanted this little trinket that he had, and ruining his life was the only way to get it."

Not every puzzle idea made it into the game.

TS: I really wanted a puzzle where you're trying to stretch a sweater by going back in time, finding a baby turtle in a pond outside, and you put the sweater on the baby turtle, and then you go 200 years in the future, and the turtle's still alive, but he's giant, and he's stretched the sweater out for you. That was my idea, but no one went for it.

Sometimes, the team had to consider that some of the game's entertaining content would be mistaken for a puzzle.

TS in the *Remastered* Developer's Commentary: We always tried to let the player know when they've exhausted the character. They're like, "Look, okay, you've found it. You've found all of the entertainment we put in this character—it's done."

DG in the *Remastered* Developer's Commentary: 'Cause people will explore as deep as you give them. It becomes a responsibility. "Oh, I've got to see if there's something down there that I'm missing." So you don't want to make it too huge.

TS in the *Remastered* Developer's Commentary: Yeah, it's an interesting thing to wrestle with. You want to put a lot in: "Well, the player might go here, they might go here, they might choose this, let's put interesting stuff in all those places." But then if you approach it in the wrong way, sometimes the player gets there and they're like, "Oh god, I've got to go through all this stuff!" and they feel like they need to find every nook and cranny in the dialogue. And you just put it in there so they'd have a variety of things to choose from, but they feel like it's a task list and they have to find it all.

TS on DGC Podcast: Every time I design a puzzle I think of, okay, there's a door, and it's locked, and there's a key right next to it—obviously that key is not gonna work in that door. There's an obvious solution to every puzzle, and we purposefully make that one not work. But we try to think about the player. "Obviously they're gonna try the key, so I've got to write a really good line that covers that." A lot of playtesting was, "Hey, tell us the puzzle solutions you tried that didn't work." And we tried to either make them work or write a good dialogue line for that. And that's the craft of making adventure games, is how many of those you can catch.

DG on DGC Podcast: That was a specific part of the process for me toward the end: Make a list of everything you can hold in your hands and make another list of everything you can touch, and compare them to figure out, "People might try this, they might try that," and try and write lines for as many of those as possible. I always want to reward the player for good thinking. If they hit on a solution for a puzzle that's not the one, I want to use that as a moment to try and guide them toward the correct solution. "All right, that wasn't quite right," but here's why! And hopefully that information will get you on the right path.

TS on DGC Podcast: That's always my defense about adventure games. When people are like, "That game's too hard. I got stuck. A lot of irrational puzzles." And I bet in any well-made adventure game, if you talk to a lot of characters and do a lot of the dialogue and try a lot of the objects, even the wrong objects, occasionally a new signpost will pop up and point you back to the path. And that's part of the gameplay experience: digging around for clues.

·

Adventure Games as Improv

Ask a fan what they love about DotT, *and one of the first things they'll mention is the game's wild sense of humor, which came straight from the minds of Schafer and Grossman.*

TS in a 2006 interview with Computer Gaming World: I feel that games are inherently funny. Because you have this totally out-of-control, improvising actor on the stage: the player. And you're trying to write dialogue and script behavior for all of the other poor actors who have to share the stage with him. And if that player actor wants to jump on your head or punch you or drive over you with his car, you need to come up with a response or some set of rules that will help the supporting actor come up with his or her own response. And for me, it's much easier to improv comedy than drama. It's really hard to come up with a meaningful, dramatic reaction to the player when he jumps on your head.

Larry Ahern [Lead Artist, *DotT*]: The story I heard about when Tim and Dave were working on the first Monkey Island game was they were scripting the whole thing and writing what they thought was placeholder dialogue, so they were being really goofy with what they had written, because the assumption they made based on reading Ron's treatment of the story was that it was going to be a little bit more serious than that. And, Ron ended up liking the stuff they wrote so much, he was like, "No, just go nuts, do it like that."

Coming up with the funniest idea often took work, but the pair knew a good one when they found it.

DG in a 2014 interview with Retrogamer.net: We tossed around ideas for what he'd use for the individual chambers. Someone suggested portable toilets, and Tim said it would be called the 'Chron-O-John,' and we all laughed our heads off and we knew we wouldn't have to think about any other ideas. Once we'd arrived at the use of portable toilets, flushing things through time seemed sort of obvious.

DG: A thing that I think reflects my sensibilities is the one-sided conversation that Hoagie has with Dead Cousin Ted about his hat. I very much like character humor over one-liners, and that whole thing is just this endless, it just goes on and on and on, and the overarching gag is just Hoagie not really realizing that this guy is dead and is not going to talk back to him, and his ability to just carry the conversation on on his own. And it's completely optional. You can play the entire game and not even click on that guy to talk to him, but it's just some optional fun for you to explore as far as you want, and that sort of breathes a little life into Hoagie as a person.

One memorable part in the game happens when the misguided Maniac Mansion *TV show becomes an important plot point. In the world of* Day of the Tentacle, *the events of* Maniac Mansion *actually happened, and Dr. Fred's story became both the popular LucasArts adventure game and the TV series that exists in our reality. He didn't get a dime for the TV series—perhaps a reflection of the game creators' own experience—and forgot to sign the LucasArts royalty contract in time, which is why Fred's been making ends meet by renting out his mansion as a hotel.*

TS: We had an experience of hearing that there was going to be a TV show, and having someone come and pitch it to us. And we could tell when they were pitching it to us that, this is not going to be right, because he's like, "Well, it's a very eccentric family, but there's a lot of love there." I was like, "All of this does not sound like the Edisons."

The very Canadian TV series—which aired in the United States on The Family Channel—had a lot of talent behind it, with the very funny Joe Flaherty starring as Dr. Fred Edison, and many other members of the legendary sketch show SCTV taking on creative roles. Future Schitt's Creek *star Eugene Levy—formerly known by most Americans as "the dad from* American Pie*"—gets the "created by" credit, and even guest-stars on an episode. But anyone who expected the TV adaptation to play out anything like the game was in for a rude awakening, as the tone and cast of characters stood in stark contrast to the source material. Dr. Fred existed as the only video game character portrayed in the show, and the episodes deal with the trials of a heartwarmingly off-kilter family rather than teen rescue missions.*

Viewers only need to hear the TV series's theme song to understand how different it is from the source material: It's more akin to the sleepy opening from something like Growing Pains *than the gritty, toe-tapping intro song of the video game. Despite running for a moderately successful three seasons and 66 episodes,* Maniac Mansion *has never seen a proper home release, and isn't available to watch legally on any streaming network as of this writing. And by the time* Day of the Tentacle *launched in June of 1993, the TV adaptation had just aired its last episode a few months earlier—making it a very recent memory in the minds of players.*

DG: I don't think any of us liked it very much. We didn't think it was very good. Obviously, we are biased about this, and we had some expectations about, here's what *Maniac Mansion* is about, and you would expect that they would have kept more of that in there. So, I don't know if we were really able to judge it dispassionately on its actual merits. But, we watched it, and, A) this doesn't feel like *Maniac Mansion*, and B) outside of that, it just doesn't seem very funny. I don't know. [...] That group of people have done many funny things, and I just don't think that that show is among them. I would be interested to have been a fly on the wall for the creative process from the beginning, where somebody decided it was a good idea to make a TV show out of *Maniac Mansion*, through all the inevitable changes that they must have made, "Oh, let's keep this and that and not any of this other stuff, and kind of do our own thing with it." So, when we were figuring out the plot for *Tentacle*, it just came up and fit in neatly. Any opportunity we have to make fun of something, we'll take.

Though the Maniac Mansion *TV series kept Dr. Fred, the recasting of his entire family drastically changed the Edison clan seen in the video game. His wife, previously a perverted old crone in the LucasArts adventure, was transformed into a put-upon but endlessly forgiving photogenic sitcom spouse played by Deborah Thacker—a Canadian actress then in her mid-20s.*

TS: It's the kind of thing where, if you didn't know about *Day of the Tentacle* or *Maniac Mansion*, it probably wouldn't have seemed as bad, but when you know that Nurse Edna—she seems kind of like a sex maniac in certain ways. She's kind of lecherous and predatory, and then you see [Fred's wife on the TV show], and she's young, attractive. Totally not like Nurse Edna. It was just funny how different it was, and we were just laughing at the process and the system, the Hollywood system, and how it changes things.

While the Maniac Mansion *TV adaptation contains some inspired touches from admittedly funny writers—no other sitcom of the era featured a human/fly hybrid as one of the principal cast members—it still had to sell itself as a marketable sitcom. That Tim Schafer was critical of the show's humor is no surprise: The show as a whole lacks the snappy, subversive comedy that's become a hallmark of his work.*

DG: When I'm playing [the game], whenever I am talking to Ben Franklin about anything, I feel Tim oozing out of his mouth. Franklin is just an over-the-top hilarious character of the sort I think only Tim could write that way. He's just, he's off in his own Franklin-y space and misunderstanding things that you say to him and delivering hilarious lines of dialogue with every breath and just generally elevating the mood around him in a magical way, and I think that is one of Tim's superpowers, is to do that. He can just, if you're around him in person, he can be funny very fast. He's a witty guy and will come up with a one-liner while you're still hearing the thing that the person said before him. And there's a reason why they have him hosting the Choice Awards at the Game Developers Conference and things like this, is that he's just sort of, he's just got this funniness to him that's immediate.

•

Hearing Voices

In 1993, the prospect of a "talkie" video game was still a novel idea. (This newly evolving medium wasn't shy about resurrecting the old-timey term, which once informed filmgoers that their formerly silent motion pictures now featured the magic of synchronized sound.) LucasArts first experimented with this idea by adding voice work to 1992's Indiana Jones and the Fate of Atlantis *in an enhanced CD-ROM version released just one month before* Day of the Tentacle. *Turning DotT into a "talkie" happened midway through production, bringing talented voice actors like Nick Jameson and Danny Delk on board—not to mention* WKRP in Cincinnati's *Richard Sanders as Bernard.*

TS: Everybody was gung-ho for CD-ROM. So, we're like, "Let's get on that train." So, I think we felt that, if [the CD-ROM install base] was not huge it was growing, and it seemed like *Day of the Tentacle*—I don't have the actual numbers—but it seems like it sold more than the Monkey Island games. It's not like making a Kinect game now, where it feels like "that's really small." It was a small but growing market, so it didn't feel like a small market.

DG: [Voiced dialogue] became a priority in the middle of the project. When we started, there was not enough of an install base of CD-ROM drives to justify doing that, and over the course of the following nine months a lot of them got sold, and I think one or two other companies started making noise about how they were going to do talkies. And, again, [general manager of LucasArts] Kelly Flock came into our office one day, and he said, "Look, we're not going to make Christmas, and I think you should make this game a talkie. How do you feel about that?" "Uh, okay. Well, if you're giving us a little extra time to finish it up, then great, we'll do it. It sounds fun." The decision [to add voiced dialogue] was just made by somebody looking at the numbers of sales of CD-ROM drives and what was in the common household, and deciding that, yeah, this was a thing we should go after.

In keeping with the legacy of classic cartoons, the supporting cast leans on impressions of celebrities and popular fictional characters as efficient shorthand for their characterization. In the past, for example, Thomas Jefferson is voiced like a dense Dudley Do-Right, John Hancock whines in the nebbish style of Woody Allen, and George Washington patronizes you with a pompous take on the self-important Thurston Howell III from Gilligan's Island.

TS: At the time, we didn't like [the voice work's reliance on celebrity/character impressions], because sometimes they seemed like broad caricatures and stereotypes. But I understand why it's done, because you're trying to differentiate all the voices and not have everyone just sound the same, so I think a really quick way to differentiate the voices is just put them in these extremes. Give you a Boston accent, a Brooklyn accent, instead of going into more nuanced characterizations. But it is a cartoon, and

I think cartoons are about being broad visually and I think being broad in the vocal styles makes sense too.

DG: There's actually a big difference between writing for a voice versus writing things to be read. There are some things about how the diction works that can really trip up an actor if you write something difficult, like, you kind of have to mouth it and make sure that it's going to work. If you can't say it, it's going to be hard for the actor to say it. And then, there's also a consideration of length. When you're hearing something, you have a less tolerance for it to go on and on and on. And an example of that is: Two previous games, *Monkey Island 1* and *2*, eventually did get voiced for special editions, and all the dialogue feels really, really long when you listen to it that way. There's [a difference between] the parts of your brain that are involved in processing written text versus listening to speech.

TS: I feel like we were always kind of reading our dialogue to ourselves anyway, because I feel like that's a good practice for good writing in general, even if it's not going to be read out loud, you should say the words out loud to see if any character actually would ever say that. So, I feel like we were already doing that, and I think sometime in the studio, the actors will make changes. They'll be like, "No one would ever say that, I can't put out that sentence."

TS: [Casting Richard Sanders as Bernard] was kind of a surprise. We were talking to [LucasArts voice acting director Tamlynn Niglio], and she was like, "Let's go over the list and tell me what you think of each voice, and what you think they sound like." "Bernard is kind of a nerd. You know, like on *WKRP in Cincinnati*, Les Nessman, kind of a nerdy guy, Les Nessman-like." And Tamlynn was like, "Well, we should see if we can get Les Nessman. The show's not on anymore—he's probably available." And I was like, "What?" At the time, it was not assumed that you can get name talent.

Though the use of costly licensed music doomed WKRP in Cincinnati *to obscurity (and off of streaming platforms), TV viewers of the late 70s and early 80s remember Sanders' portrayal of Les Nessman as a sweeter George Costanza—ineffectual, balding, bespectacled, and prone to injury. In other words, the perfect personality to project onto Bernard. And Nessman was actually fresh in the minds of* Day of the Tentacle *players; after becoming a smash hit in the world of reruns, the series returned for a 1991–1993 reboot uncreatively titled* The New WKRP in Cincinnati *(and this series aired its final episode just a month before* DotT's *release). Some cast members didn't return, but Sanders reprised his role from a decade earlier.*

TS: It was [after we started developing the game] when FMV started becoming a thing. So, the idea of using someone whose name we recognized. That started this whole thing, which still, the process we go through today, with *Brutal Legend*, we're like, "We want kind of a Jack Black kind of character." And someone said, "What if we actually got Jack?" It seems impossible, and then it works out, and you can't imagine it going any other way.

The game came out as both a CD-ROM and on floppy disk. It was a struggle to get the whole game to fit on the older format.

DG: We got sort of towards the end, and we had gotten to the point where we made the decision to have it be a talkie game. And, when we were sort of getting near to launch, then the subject came up of, alright, we need to fit this on floppies for the floppy version. And, yeah, we did have a hard limit of, I believe it was six. I said, it's got to fit on these six floppies, because, we did the math and the economics, and we're going to lose money if we don't do that.

So, it actually was part of my personal job to get it to fit on these six floppies, and, we had made the decision early on that we knew that all of the recorded dialogue was not going to fit onto the floppies, so we would just do the opening and the rest would be text only, like all the games had been up until then. And I was literally taking the few, the sound effects, we still had sound effects and stuff, and, individual lines of dialogue, and recompressing them at a lower data rate to shave a few kilobytes off the overall file size, to squeeze things in to the six floppies, because we were a little over. And that process actually took weeks, if I remember correctly.

And, as I said, a third of our audience was in Germany, and literally, when we translated the text into German, it didn't fit on the six floppies anymore. So, in Germany, it shipped on seven floppies.

Still, the floppy version had to make a few compromises.

TS: We had to do things like, we decided, we wanted to put voice in, but that wasn't going to work for floppy, but we really wanted to do it, so we actually did just voice for the intro to the game and compressed it a lot. So, if you play it on floppy, there's this hissy version of the voice in it. The thought was, you could imagine the voice the rest of the time, from the character they're supposed to be. I don't know. Looking back, it seems like you could have left [all the dialogue as] text.

•

Back to Going Back to the Mansion

Schafer and Grossman briefly considered making a third game in the MM series.

TS: Me and Dave always had ideas for another [Maniac Mansion] game, but I think those characters seemed pretty happy where they were at the end of this story, and I don't feel like there's other stories to tell.

DG: I think the experience was remarkably formative for me as a game developer. Certainly, by the time we did that project, I understood some things about game design and story. I'm always learning new stuff about that—I still am. That was the first experience with trying to lead a team and trying to bring something to life from the top. So, yeah, I think that was a super important experience for me as a designer. It was only my third game, and the first one I was more or less in charge of. And, just in terms of the final product, I still think it's one of the best things I've ever done. It holds together really well and does what it set out to do very effectively. For all of its cracks and crannies, I think it's something that came out really well.

TS: Such a special thing about [the original] *Maniac Mansion* is that it's this little tight compact little Rubik's Cube, of a three-by-three little environment—you just twist and go around in different directions and angles and see all the different sides of it. But definitely, I think that led to criticism of the game when it came out as being too short. And I don't think it is shorter than lots of [other] adventure games, but it definitely feels shorter because it's in one location.

The main reward when you're playing an adventure game is a new piece of background art. You solve a puzzle and you get into a new room. And I think people, whether they realize that or not, are basing their progress in the game and their excitement on, *How long ago was it the last time I walked into a new room?*

And, with *Day of the Tentacle*, there's so much more going on with the puzzles and the characters; it doesn't really need that. Some people might want to go on these big epics. But I think what's special about *DotT* [is] that it's not this big epic journey across the land. It's tight. It's this one focused little point.

DAY OF THE TENTACLE

ART

IF YOU LOOK AT THE ANIMATION landscape of 1993, the cartoony nature of *Day of the Tentacle* should make perfect sense.

Of course, the creative minds behind *Maniac Mansion*'s sequel clearly drew from the cartoons of their childhoods (or, more accurately, their parents' childhoods), but during the time of *DotT*'s production, American animation made for television found itself in a short-lived Renaissance of sorts. In a movement spurred on by pioneers like Ralph Bakshi, Steven Spielberg, and The Walt Disney Company, the crass, cheaply-made TV cartoons of the 80s and earlier slowly transitioned into high-quality productions meant to achieve more than selling toys. Animated programs like *Tiny Toon Adventures*, *Animaniacs*, and *The Ren & Stimpy Show* existed as expensive throwbacks to the golden age of cinematic cartoons, making good animation en vogue again after decades of ignominy.

This period of newfound relevance birthed *Day of the Tentacle*, a game that aspired to capture the same spirit as classic, cinematic cartoons—despite the constraints of an extremely low resolution and needing the game to fit onto six floppy discs.

•

Starting at LucasArts

While lead artists Peter Chan and Larry Ahern were no strangers to the LucasArts process—having both worked on Monkey Island 2: LeChuck's Revenge—*the sheer ambition of* Day of the Tentacle *made for a real learning experience, with increased responsibilities and new challenges for the two artists.*

LA: The first project I worked on when I got [to LucasArts]... I was hired in 1990, and I was really interested in the comedy games, and then, they went around and asked all the new people, "What would you like to work on?" And they were about to do the sequel to *Monkey Island*, and I said, "I want to do that." And they said, "Okay, great, but you're the new guy, so you're going to work on *The Dig*." So, I ended up on that.

The Dig went through various revisions and would eventually see a release in 1995.

PC: I was in-house [at LucasArts] for three adventure games: *Monkey Island, Day of the Tentacle,* and *Full Throttle.* The reason why my name is on other games was just because I always brought my lunch to work, so, during my lunch break, I would just walk around and ask if anyone needed any help. It was just a way of learning. I treated LucasArts like a university, I just took advantage of the facility and the projects, just to educate myself and learn basically.

So, for me, taking on that role was really scary. When I first came on, I was green. I was right out of school, plus I had primarily never played video games. So here I was, my first job was *Monkey Island 2,* and they had already started, and I remember Ron Gilbert giving me an assignment. It was part of my test, to see whether or not I was good enough to be part of the team.

LA: [*The Dig*] ended up getting shelved about six months in, and I got to switch to working on *Monkey Island 2* midstream. At that point I was working with Tim [Schafer] and Dave [Grossman], and I guess Ron Gilbert was the project leader. He would come and give the animators a list of things to animate. "Give me [Monkey Island protagonist] Guybrush picking this thing up, or leaning down, or falling down," or whatever. And he wouldn't give any context for it. And I tried asking questions about it, and he said, "Just do this, this, this, and this, laundry list, check it off," and I got real frustrated with that. So, I started wandering over to Tim and Dave's office, and saying, "Hey, so, what do you need this for? What's happening?" Then they'd describe the scene for me, and I'd say, "Oh, well, wouldn't it be more fun if I did it this way?" And they'd go, "Yeah, that'd be even better. Go do that." And I'm like, "Okay, can you get it approved with Ron, then?" "Oh, don't worry, we'll take care of that."

PC: [LucasArts] was small in comparison to [game companies] nowadays. Yes, it was very, very small. I mean, Ron and Tim were the project leads so I always had to get their approvals, but there were opportunities for collaboration, and for me to design something that wasn't exactly in the document. Back then, I don't think we really had art directors or production designers. Those were usually titles for film. And then, for us, I think because it was so new, "lead artist" just meant the guy who was stuck doing most of the art.

LA: So then, when it was time to do the next project, and they started on *Day of the Tentacle*, [Tim and Dave] had been working with Ron and Gary Winnick, who had done the original *Maniac Mansion*, working with them on concepts and stuff, and then they started pulling a team together, and I wanted to be involved with that. I had done a lot of cartooning in the past, so I wanted to do character designs. And then Peter Chan was going to be the background artist, so he and I got to work together and figure out a look for the whole thing.

PC: Luckily, I had [Sam & Max creator Steve Purcell] there during *Monkey Island 2*. But after *Monkey 2* I was given the opportunity to work on adventure games with Tim, and that's when I started to get really scared and nervous and insecure. Because now I'm given this role to come up with something brand new. When I came on to work on *Monkey 2*, basically they told me the art style was established already. The art style was, let's say, the Disney film, *Pinocchio*. So, it was like, okay, I can kind of mimic that. That was easy because someone already came up with that idea. So for me to try to figure out what *Day of the Tentacle* was going to look like was, at first, a great opportunity, but, sometimes, it's too wide open. You kind of have to figure out, okay, what's the best style for this wacky game?

•

Capturing Cartooniness

With their new roles on Maniac Mansion*'s sequel, both Chan and Ahern had an amazing degree of freedom in determining the visual style for* Day of the Tentacle.

With the basic concept for the game in front of them, the two found inspiration in the same source—an animation legend.

LA: Another frustration I had experienced working on *Monkey Island 2* was this feeling that the different artists that were working on things were not doing one consistent style. It's like each individual artist would kind of do what they thought their version of a Monkey Island character should look like, and there was nobody officially art directing it and coming in and saying, "No, that character's off-model, or that needs to look more like this." So, I felt like there were a lot of frustrating stylistic changes depending on the scene you were in.

And so I talked about, okay, if I'm going to work as an animator on *Day of the Tentacle*, I really want to be able to have the authority to pull everything together and make it consistent. We should come up with character designs, and those are locked down. This is a process. We figure out what these characters are in advance, and then make sure it all matches stylistically, and then everybody animates those characters—as opposed to bringing someone in later and saying, "Oh, design the character you're going to animate," and hope it matches.

DG: Peter was making an art style, and Larry was designing characters. And all of us loved these Chuck Jones cartoons. I remember Larry from early on saying,

"We need to have more squashing and stretching with the characters in our games." He felt that as a general thing, not just for this game, but that they should all have that, because it's expressive and fun. There was a certain applicability to that to the kinds of ridiculous moments that we were always thinking about when we designed these games.

LA: Every time I got a scene that was supposed to be just some generic thing, I was always pushing for, "What's the context of the scene, can we turn this into something entertaining in and of itself, as opposed to just functionally? Is he functionally picking up the banana, or is he picking up the banana and the banana pops out of the peel, and the peel drops, and he slips on it? What are we trying to do in this scene?" I wanted to have some fun with it, because no one was letting me write or design anything, so, it's like, "If this is my area, what can I do with it?"

I was always pushing at the seams on that kind of stuff, trying to get Ron to agree to let me do something crazier and crazier. And he always pushed back. Part of that [preference] too was realizing, at that point, I don't think we had ever seen a game that had been done [in a ridiculous cartoon] kind of style. Things were all just sort of generic, or, a lot of games tried to take themselves more seriously, sword and sorcery types of things.

Peter Chan: [My son] was born, and I remember watching cartoons with him. It was Saturday morning stuff: Chuck Jones, "Duck Dodgers," and "What's Opera, Doc?" And I remember looking at it, and going, "There's something there," and then I had to do some research. And back in those days you couldn't just Google something and find all these images. There wasn't any, except for a few books that were out there. So back in those days, you had to go out and buy books and then get the reference from it.

And so I had to look up anything that had to do with Bugs Bunny, Warner Bros. stuff, and I found reference material of Chuck Jones's art director back then, Maurice Noble. So, I just looked at the handful of images that was in the book and just studied them, and I watched the cartoons on VHS, trying to pause certain shots so I could study the layouts on TV. When you pause on a VHS, you get all these lines on TV screens, so it's really hard to see. That's how we studied. From there, whatever went through my head and came out of my arm was basically the style for the game.

LA: I was really pushing for [one consistent art style], and then, out of frustration from working on Monkey Island, the characters were so small, especially their faces, it was really hard to do much of anything in terms of facial expressions on those characters. So I was wanting to push the look of *Day of the Tentacle* in a more cartoony direction with large heads and big googly eyes so you can see the whites of their eyes, because they're so much more expressive that way. And, I guess the original *Maniac Mansion* did have larger heads on the characters too, so it was probably a little bit leaning in that direction. At that time, there was a limit to the amount of pixels you could move around on the screen for a character. So we were given basically the maximum pixel height of a character, or maybe it was a pixel volume kind of thing.

DG: I feel like it was Peter who really put a nail in that, and said, "Let's use Chuck Jones as an inspiration and go from there." I think he was just thinking about it and said, "This is what seems like would be appropriate to me, and I'll do these sparse backgrounds, and I'll do this and do that, and it'll all feel like a cartoon." We're like, "Yeah, that's great." And we, in turn, will be inspired by that, and there was a lot of back and forth between, oh, now we're writing these things that feel like that, and that would influence the art. I would do dialogue, and I would be influenced by what the characters looked like. It came up organically, and once we knew that was where we were going, it was easy for us all to go there together.

PC: I wasn't trying to flat-out do a classic [Warner Bros. background artist] Maurice Noble layout, or art style. It was inspired by him, but it was basically what Larry and I kind of chose and put together. I was looking up at Larry, too, I was impressed by all these amazing people at LucasArts. So, I looked at Larry and he was on his way to designing these characters, and I thought, "Oh my God, I've got to create environments for his awesome characters to live in." And so, I had to find that happy balance for everything to come together.

LA: So, that was part of the challenge: Figuring out how do you get the expressive character that you want within those limitations. So, I kind of worked on character designs based on that. What could I do, giving them larger heads, bigger eyes, and expressive faces, and still have it look like one consistent style. Early on it was just Peter and I working on the visual look for things. We did a lot of tests where we did some background mockups. We'd put some characters in it, we'd figure out how the backgrounds needed to be done so they didn't get too busy and compete with the characters, because a lot of time a character walking around a real complex background can get totally lost—and some of that's the background and some of that's the character.

PC: We were able to share the game with Chuck Jones down the road, and he was very kind. He had a lot of nice things to say about the game.

TS: We met Chuck Jones, we brought him in to look at the game, and we were hoping he would say something we could use as a blurb on the front of the box, but he never did. He was like, "Nice, cool." His actual advice was, "Have you thought about making the characters not human? Because you can get away with a lot more craziness if they're not human." When their faces are human, you expect them to look good, or to emote in a human way, but if they're rabbits you can change it all up.

Day of the Tentacle **composer, Peter McConnell:** About that time, Chuck Jones visited to give us a lecture. And he saw Peter's stuff, and he said, "You've got to come work for me." But I guess Peter liked the independence a little bit better, so he stuck with us, fortunately for us. Which gives you a sense of how excited we all were about what we were doing. [Video games were] an exciting new frontier to be working on.

And Chuck Jones wasn't the only creative superstar to check in on Day of the Tentacle's *development.*

Tim Schafer on a 2012 episode of the podcast, *Retronauts:* We did our first real pass at actual planning,

I think, for [*Day of the Tentacle*]. Maybe it just didn't seem like *Monkey* [*Island*] 1 or 2 were planned because Ron [Gilbert] would just tell us what we were doing— sometimes that day. Like, "I've got a new piece of background art for you; put it in." After that, we did storyboards for every single background in the game. We'd never had the whole game to look at before. And then, we had it all on the wall, and then George Lucas came in—one of the three times I ever saw George Lucas. I was all excited; I said, "Look, we storyboarded!" And he's like, "Yeah, it's hard to make a movie without a script."

•

Wrestling with Technology

Finding the art style for Day of the Tentacle *posed one problem for Chan and Ahern; communicating it through the technology of 1993 was a different problem altogether. Working with a 320 x 200 resolution, the two artists needed to employ some creative solutions to make* Day of the Tentacle *evoke the feeling of a classic Warner Bros. cartoon while still fitting the game onto six floppy discs.*

LA: I did everything on paper, and then I would do an initial scan. But back in those days, line drawings at that resolution just kind of went to crap. So, it was mostly done to get a silhouette, because you couldn't use any of the line work—it was just a starting point to get the proportions. And then I'd go basically redraw from that on the computer, and figure out the basic shape of the character, and then start dropping in the color.

And then [I] pretty much started with the main characters, probably did the front view and profile pretty early. The first [animation] I would have done, then, would have been the walk cycle. So, all this stuff is the early design pre-production phase, just figuring out what's going to work, doing a lot of testing. But once that direction seemed like it was going to work, then we had the design document that had all the lists of characters, and I just started cranking out character designs for all the different people that were going to be in the game. People and tentacles.

Instead of trying to draw backgrounds digitally, Chan cleverly used markers to create background art that could then be scanned in.

Peter Chan: Back in those days, [it was my] first time drawing with a mouse. I'm a traditional guy, so I like to draw with a pencil. So for me to try to draw with a potato in my hand, and then, look up on a screen, and the pixels are the size of coasters: It was very difficult. Thankfully, when I came out of school, I started working at an advertising agency, so that's how I started learning how to do things in markers. So I got pretty prolific with marker technique, in drawing with markers, and it was fast.

Larry Ahern: I think we hated [the technology] at the time. Because we felt like, [art] is a real thing, and you are tying my hands behind my back and making me stand on one foot to do it. So, I think the farther into it you get, and maybe the more distance you get from it, and you have perspective to look back on it. Then it's easier to say, "Wow, that really was a certain skill set we had to have—there's a design process." I would liken it to illustrative graphic design. It's sort of like, it's not going to be an oil painting, but you're trying to take the core visual idea of an image and simplify it into a logo and a graphic design element. So it's still pictorial, but it's a different way of doing something pictorial.

We used to joke that we're learning to become mosaic artists, and I was actually pushing the company when we moved to our new bigger offices, I think it was around '95, '96, I was saying, we need to put mosaic tiles in an entryway with our characters, and make it so if you walk over it you can't really tell, it's so big, but then if you have a vantage point from a balcony somewhere where you can look down and realize, oh my God, it's giant pixel versions of our characters.

PC: Scanning started to surface, and the scanning machine was this big expensive machine, and no one really knew how to do it and use it and take advantage of it, and I remember I was really intimidated by this scanner. But the good thing was, I was able to draw everything traditionally, do the marker version of it, and then scan it into the computer. And then once it's scanned in, all the colors are in there, but the problem is, it totally pixelates. It just turns into this mosaic of pixels, and so then I would have to spend time cleaning it up as best as I can, just to make it look cleaner.

Chan is referring to compression artifacts, flaws that happen when images are digitized in a way that prohibits them from taking up too much disk space. This issue transforms areas of an original piece of artwork into large blocks of color, requiring an artist to restore some of the lost nuance to the digital version.

Dave Grossman on a 2012 episode of the podcast, *Retronauts*: During *Monkey* [*Island*] 2, we got *the* scanner. It was way more expensive than my car. I think the thing cost $10,000. And it was one of these flatbed scanners you can get at the supermarket now for about 50 bucks. You had to be checked out on the scanner in order to use it, in case some clown broke it. And you had to book time on it. All artists were all about it during the day, so you couldn't use it [then]. So I would stay after work because I wanted to scan stuff to make, you know, a little desktop background for my Mac.

LA: At the time I remember we were very frustrated with [our tools], but one of the projects that I did was kind of a blast. It showed the complete torment and then the joy that you get from figuring it out. I actually did characters for the bonus level in [the 1993 LucasArts game for SNES and Genesis] *Zombies Ate My Neighbors*, and when you get to that bonus level at the end of the game, it unlocks a level that's the offices of LucasArts, and we put desks in there and had caricatures of every one of the employees sitting in there. I guess a couple of artists had taken a stab at trying to do that, and they were struggling, and so Mike Ebert, the project leader on that, came up to me—and I was in between projects—and he said, "Hey, you want to take a stab at doing some caricatures of everybody in the building?" And, the deal was, unlike *Day of the Tentacle*, where it's like 15 x 20 pixels for their giant heads, these were smaller Nintendo characters, and I think it was like eight by eight, or something like that.

And he's like, "Yeah, take a shot at it, see if you can figure it out." And I spent a couple hours in the morning just hammering on it, and I couldn't for the life of me figure it out. And then, all of a sudden, something clicked, I just got to the point where I realized, with these few pixels, there's only, like, four potential noses that you can make, and five possible head shapes. It was basically, there's only so many ways you can do it, but if you have three to five heads, eyes, noses, mouths, whatever, if you have a couple of each, you can recombine any of those in a certain way, and you can make Bob or Sam or Bill or whoever.

PC: Because I didn't play games, I didn't know the limitations: what to pick up, what the players could pick up and not use, and I didn't know anything about gameplay. All I was doing was drawing pretty pictures, according to what Tim and Dave needed for the room. And so, because I didn't know gameplay, I would always put things in the foreground and the middle ground, all these yummy things to pick up. And, I remember doing the drawing, and then walking across the parking lot into Dave and Tim's office and saying, "How's this look?" And, I think it took many rounds, but Dave and Tim were very patient with me, and they would say, "Peter, you can't do that, and put all this stuff in the foreground and middle ground, because people will want to pick these things up." So, it was hard for me because I wanted to populate the drawing with props and things like that that I thought would be interesting.

That was a learning curve for me to pull back and simplify, and it finally clicked, okay, I get it. That's why a lot of the foreground I just turned black, just so I can create some depth in the drawing or in the room. But then it was an obvious cue that you couldn't pick up any of those props, because they were black silhouettes. But it was just an excuse to try to create some depth in such a flat environment.

Meanwhile, working on a game with one setting in three distinct timelines presented its own difficulties.

PC: The challenge was basically taking a room and then having to do three versions of it, because of the time travel. So, trying to keep things consistent in layout, but then change the subject matter each time.

For players, though, the game's great art and animation more than made up for the technical limitations of the time.

DG in the *Remastered* Developer's Commentary: There is no lip-syncing. Which is funny because I've gotten many compliments on the lip-syncing. [...] If there's pauses in the audio, it stops moving the lips.

•

Starting with a Bang

Even 23 years later, Day of the Tentacle*'s cinematic opening is still a showstopper. Every element of this four-minute prologue—including the animation, music, sound effects, and jokes—ushered in a new era of excellence for LucasArts, and completely sold the experience as an interactive cartoon. Communicating this expressive chunk of* DotT *via the technology of 1993, however, took some work.*

LA: A lot of [the inspiration behind *DotT*'s opening involved] looking at previous games we had worked on and realizing, God, we put the credits at the front partially because the games are so crazy long, who knows if people ever see your name in lights. Like the old movies, credits at the front. But after a while, the team started getting bigger, and it just started feeling like, "I'm sitting through a bunch of still frame pictures with names on it. This is boring." You don't want a bunch of little pixelated characters walking around the bottom of the screen while the credits are rolling, because that's just not going to cut it. You want to do something impactful. This was an offshoot of our exploration of what we could do graphically and stylistically, realizing that, you know what, if we keep the colors in our environments simpler, we can do more.

DotT's *non-interactive intro employs a lot of the graphical tricks from this era before the CD-ROM format became mandatory and pre-rendered sequences made for an effective solution to the game's tight size limitations. In the establishing bits of this four-minute scene, we see glorious close-ups of characters that offer very few actual moving parts—and when these parts do move, it's in a fairly choppy manner. Once our central cast gets their mission and piles into Bernard's jalopy for a journey to the Edison mansion, the real graphical showcase begins as the opening credits roll.*

In what amounts to ten different shots, this sequence portrays the car zipping, bending, and jumping across the asphalt, causing plenty of property damage along the way. (And picking up an unwitting cow as a passenger.) It's a sequence that could easily be done today, but given the amount of space the developers had to work with, devoting so many assets to a functionally unimportant (and skippable) credits sequence feels incredibly bold. Of course, the big cheat here is that all of these smooth animations play out in pure silhouette—drastically shrinking the amount of memory they would otherwise occupy. The result is what, to the 1993 player, looks like a full-screen cartoon, and in an era where watching pre-rendered videos within a tiny QuickTime window on your monitor felt like the height of human technological achievement.

PC: We hired a hotshot from CalArts named Kyle Balda. I think he was still in school, and he was just an intern. So, this young guy comes in and we give him something to do... but I remember the reason why the intro looks so good is Kyle. He did all that beautiful animation in the intro. And so, it was just a great exercise in trying to simplify the environments down so he can put in the animation without it being chunky. And so I had to turn everything into a nice monochromatic nighttime scene.

Kyle Balda later went on to be an animator for Pixar, and eventually moved to Illumination Entertainment, where he directed the staggeringly popular Minions, Despicable Me 3, *and* Minions: The Rise of Gru. *It shouldn't be surprising that that person responsible for putting together one of the most memorable video game intros ever made is also responsible for some of the most popular and profitable animated movies in history.*

DG: There always was this idea that the first few minutes of the game are going to set expectations and are going to help you sell. And you've got to make demos, and that's usually the piece that you show. So, typically, a lot of attention gets put into the first few minutes and the last few minutes of the game. In this one, we definitely concentrated all up front. In fact, it used to be even bigger, and, partly that was just inexperience on our part about how to best set up a story and what you needed to know. There was a lot of expositional stuff that we had to take care of to get you to that mansion with some particular goals in mind.

And, I think [the opening] was seven minutes originally, and it was [LucasArts game designer] Hal Barwood who played through it and said, "Guys, this is just too long. You have to cut it somewhere." So, we cut it in half. That whole part where you first arrive at the mansion and you split up, and one of you goes upstairs and one of you goes downstairs, and you go find the tentacles. You basically just go and you find them and free them, and that's all you do in that section. It was just put in there to break up the giant seven-minute cutscene that we had done for the beginning, and I think it's slightly more palatable now.

The directors' gratitude to this veteran LucasArts employee can be found in the ending credits, which include the line "Opening Fixed by Hal Barwood."

•

Looking Back on *Day of the Tentacle*

LA: You've probably heard this before. I think a lot of us say this: It was one of the best games I've ever worked on. And I feel that way in terms of the experience as well as the results, which is funny, because it was very limited technology. There were a lot of things that we wanted to do that we couldn't do. But I think a lot of times you get great creative solutions to problems when you have limitations. And combine that with a small team and a relatively short development cycle—we weren't going to bite off more than we could chew. We just found ways that we could innovate, and then within the limitations that we had, we just did our best to [make] something that was fun and funny and visually interesting.

PC: All I can say is that *Day of the Tentacle* was such a learning curve for me. When I think back, I was pretty new at the company at the time. I felt like I had so much to learn, I put my head down and just tried to pick up things as quickly as I could. And I was very intimidated at the time because I wasn't a gamer and everyone else seemed to be. And so, again, I was insecure and was trying to impress, but at the same time, I was insecure, just because I didn't know anything about games. And I was surrounded by all these incredible talents and artists and animators.

This is the funny thing, and Tim teases me, but it's no secret now, but I've never played the game. I've never played any of my games that I helped design since. I didn't realize that until last year that *Day of the Tentacle* was a sequel to *Maniac Mansion*. Because I have this faint memory of designing a different kind of house, and, or mansion, and then sharing it with Tim, and I don't know if that drawing exists or not or if it is just a doodle or whatnot, but I remember they said, "No, it has to look like the house in Maniac Mansion." And it didn't even occur to me that it was a sequel. I was like, "Oh, really?"

LA: *Day of the Tentacle* was pretty focused. It was a fun team to work with, it was a small team, so everybody was very collaborative. It's a heck of a lot easier to work on stuff like that when everyone's riffing off stuff together and figuring out how to do it, and come up with great solutions. Whereas I look at *Full Throttle*—we tried to do way too much on that. If you look at a lot of individual shots, there are things that are pretty scrappy because we'd rough out an animation scene and realize, "Well, this is the scene that we want, and we need these three shots, but we hardly have any time, so let's just toss those together super fast."

When I see those, I still cringe a little bit, even though the overall impact is: Hey, that's a good scene. And then by the time we got on *Curse of Monkey Island*, it was just a huge team. That gets hard. I feel like that starts to turn into more of an assembly line. The animators on that did phenomenal work, but, trying to keep that all coordinated, I probably turned into a little bit more of a dictator than I should have. Hopefully all those guys have gone on to do bigger and better things and don't hate me...

PC: Luckily, I don't get bombarded [with *Day of the Tentacle* questions] a lot because I live on an island; I don't live in California anymore. A lot of people don't even know what I do for a living out here, and that's the way I like it. When it does happen, it's mostly when I go over to Denmark because I teach at a college there, an animation college called the Animation Workshop, and I've been doing it for eight years now. I go over there and teach concept art. So, when I'm there, that's when I get a lot of questions. Mostly from the young students. They're all in their twenties so our games were part of their childhood, part of their middle school experience. When they come up to me, it makes me feel old when they say, "Oh, yeah, when I was in the sixth grade, or when I was in the eighth grade, whatever, I played your game." Or I would hear many stories of, "I used to put tracing paper on my computer screen and try to draw your backgrounds."

And, that's when I would hear stories about *Day of the Tentacle*, or how it inspired other kids to draw, and that makes me happy, because I never thought I would be a person to inspire other people, but I remember when I was younger having those mentors or those folks

I would look up to, and I would do the same thing. I would copy.

LA: Other than kind of figuring out how to animate on the second Monkey Island game, *Day of the Tentacle*... pretty much my learning curve on animating was happening on the job. But, I was just going nuts for it. We were getting out Looney Tunes movies and freeze-framing on things to see how things were done, and getting all the reference books we could get. That was happening across the company because we had a lot of new people there as the company was growing, and we did a lot of after-work sessions studying animation and doing cartooning, and everybody was just going crazy for learning how to do this stuff.

So, there's a lot of healthy competition between projects, people trying to figure out how to do things and one-up each other. It was a point of pride. How good can we make this? And I just loved the process of learning how to do it, figuring out technical limitations: How can you get an animation to look the way you want, how can you get a character to turn out. And for me, having worked, I guess I'd been there a year and a half or so, I felt like all the previous projects I had worked on were little pixelated characters that didn't have the level of personality that I wanted to put into a character. So, this being the first game [on which] I got to design the characters, it was just a thrill.

For Ahern, the game was a chance to stretch his comedic chops like never before.

LA: The thing that I was thrilled about working on this project versus the previous two I had done [was that] Tim and Dave just kind of let me go to town on this stuff. With *Day of the Tentacle*, I was the animation director, I was putting the scenes together. They had the design and they had the script, or they had the story, and then they were going to come in later and write the dialogue. But all the conversations and dialogue, that happens later, whereas the animation happens first. So, there's a storyline of what's going to happen, but a lot of times the scenes are more about "what's the puzzle scenario?"

I'd sit down with Tim and Dave, and we'd talk about what's happening in this scene, what are you trying to do here, what's the flavor of it, how does this connect to everything else, and then, what's the puzzle? And we'd brainstorm, or sometimes it would just be three of us sitting there, trying to figure out what would be funny, or fun for the scene, and, I'd suggest ideas for, well, maybe the character can do this or that. Other times, they'd just say, "Here's the scenario, go figure something out." That was my first opportunity to actually do some writing, and technically I guess you'd call that gag writing, or joke writing. It was slapstick visual gags, but that was sort of my first taste of getting to write for games, which I went on to do a lot more of later.

You're not just animating a specific list of tasks, it was: How do you put comedy and character expression into how they're accomplishing the tasks that they need to do? So if the puzzle needs them to do X, Y, and Z, there's an interesting way to do that that's going to be appropriate for each character, and is going to have something funny about it. I loved the fact that they let me run with that stuff and figure out ways to do that, and I tried to do similar things with the other animators that worked on the project, if they had ideas for how to do the different gags.

MUSIC: AN INTERVIEW
WITH PETER
MCCONNELL

DAY OF THE TENTACLE'S *art, animation, and writing helped sell its status as an interactive cartoon, but it wouldn't reach this ambitious goal without one important piece of the puzzle: music.*

Just as Carl Stalling's scores synchronized with the movements of Bugs Bunny, Daffy Duck, and the like, DotT's *music needed to communicate action as well as atmosphere. Luckily, LucasArts had a friend in iMUSE. This proprietary system ensured the image would always sync up to the sound, and had the capability of making seamless transitions from one piece to another—impressive in an era where the "sound card" existed as an often-costly accessory, rather than something naturally included with every PC. Without a doubt, LucasArts' early innovations in the field of music made their golden age of adventures sound leagues ahead of the canned MIDI loops of PC speaker cacophony heard in other games.*

TS: Peter [McConnell] worked that way—he always works that way where he comes up with a theme per character. And then, the scenes where they come in and out, he weaves the scene in and out. Or, even when you're talking about a certain thing, in the same way that John Williams, if you talk about the Force, the Force theme comes in. Even if it's just three notes, you feel that Force theme, and when someone talks about Bernard, his theme will come in. I think it was also one of the later, one of the last big hurrahs for the iMUSE system, because that was something we worked on for Monkey Island, where we could have music that doesn't start and stop, it just evolves and changes as parts are turned on and off on a MIDI level.

I forgot about that until I was playing through the game again. I was like, I really miss this. Even though it's really lo-fi MIDI samples, I missed how the transitions always happened on the beats, and it's like a live composer was composing the score in a soundstage, and musicians were working on the fly with whatever was happening on the screen. Because, when you switch back and forth, there's always that [hums a few notes to announce a new character], or that little bit of [hums Hoagie's theme].

And then as you walk into the next room, it doesn't start and stop, but just waits until the end of the measure and then starts the new theme. It's really elegant, I think. It creates this feeling, that the entire thing is one big score. As we moved into digital soundtracks, we tended to more just crossfade or fade out and fade up digital pieces, which is great because you can have live musicians and all that, like on *Grim [Fandango]*. But I did miss that iMUSE system, and that's what we really tried to maintain with the remaster. We went back. We used better samples, nicer samples, but [iMUSE is still the engine running all of the music].

Peter McConnell served as LucasArts' in-house composer from 1991 until 2004. Odds are, if you played a PC game during this period, you've probably tapped your foot along to one of McConnell's scores—even if you didn't play adventure games. Though he and his peers' compositions remain some of the most ambitious of that era, making ancient sound hardware sing so well posed a major challenge. McConnell details his processes in an interview I conducted with him via Skype in 2016. Because he is the only composer interviewed about the game's music, his comments will appear in the form of an interview instead of an oral history.

Bob Mackey: Could you explain how *Day of the Tentacle* differed from other projects you worked on at LucasArts?

Peter McConnell: Well, *Day of the Tentacle* was the third project I did there, the first two being *Monkey [Island] 2* and *Indiana Jones and the Fate of Atlantis*. It was different in the sense that, by that time, our interactive music system had been pretty well fleshed-out, and so we were pretty good at using it. [For] all three of those—*Monkey 2*, *Indy*, and *DotT*—Michael Land and Clint Bajakian and I split the duties, and *Day of the Tentacle* was the second-to-last game. I think *TIE Fighter* might have been the last game where we split our duties equally, and didn't have one guy who was the lead composer. So, those early games, we did a lot of the scores more like being in a band than being one composer, and we would trade pieces back and forth, especially for *Monkey 2* and *Indy*, and very especially for *Monkey 2*, we would actually collaborate on some of the pieces.

By the time *DotT* came along, we were working together, but we always had our spheres of influence. Michael did the future, I mostly did the present, and Clint mostly did the past. And with one exception: I think I did a couple of pieces for the past because they were Dr. Fred pieces, and I did Dr. Fred's theme.

Full Throttle was my next [LucasArts game], and that was all me, excluding the [rock band] Gone Jackals, which, I also found for the game and kind of managed their involvement. So *DotT* was probably the last game [in which we composed as a team] where it was original music [and] we weren't working with John Williams themes or something like that.

To pick [between collaboration and being the sole composer for a game], I would pick being the sole guy, and I think a lot of people would. But, especially these days, when I work out of a home studio, and most of the time the only human beings I talk to I talk to like I'm talking to you now, I like to do a collaboration whenever the chance comes up.

I wanted to ask you about working with the technology of that era. What did the iMUSE system present in terms of challenges and, in terms of making your job potentially more interesting? And do you miss working under those limitations?

PM: Working on the music system was a big part of the draw for me for that job. I came out here, and my original plan was to do a band with [future LucasArts composer] Michael Land. He was out here first, and by the time I came out, he had gotten a job at Lucas and the band idea fell through. But, there was this really rare opportunity to, (A) get paid for writing music, which was an entirely new experience, and (B)—and notice the order I put these in—to apply the technical knowledge that I'd gained going back to starting as a physics major in college before switching to music, and [the knowledge I'd gained when I worked] at Lexicon, which is an audio company that makes reverb units.

And Michael and I both [had] worked there, and we had this opportunity to apply some of my music-computer-y skills to a brand new situation where we were inventing stuff, so that was hugely fun in the beginning and it made up for the god-awful sound that we had to work with. I know I'm somewhat committing heresy here, because there's a lot of nostalgia for the sounds of that era, and I'm still fond of the sound of the MT-32. It's got a certain quality to it that's very charming and warm, and you can do some pretty interesting music on it.

Yeah, there's a certain warmth to that SoundBlaster era that you just don't hear anymore—it's just completely gone from history.

PM: Yeah, I'm not a big fan of the FM synthesis, though, and never was. And we took it extremely seriously. We did completely different sets of music files for Sound Canvas, MT-32, AdLib, and even in the very early games like *Monkey [Island]* we even did PC Speaker, which, if you've ever done anything for PC

Speaker, the speaker goes in and it goes out. Those are the commands.

The long and the short of it is, I just did not like the sound. It was truly a case of polishing a turd, to get your music that you worked so hard on to sound remotely like a bass guitar and drums—or even more remotely like an orchestra. And it was a great cerebral musical challenge in one way, but ultimately you had to live with the fact that at the end of the day, you had something that sounded [only] slightly less awful. Not to take away from the charm of that era, because I think for a lot of people, the reason [they] look back fondly on the sound of those games is that, since you didn't have good or even okay production values, what you had to do was make things convincing and jump out of the speakers in a different way. Like, for instance, having a memorable tune.

So we all took that as our big challenge. We're going to write tunes that people are going to enjoy. Of course, you don't want to be too annoying either, that's always the dance. So, in that sense, those were the good old days, the glory days. We were like a rock and roll band, we were writing tunes together, we were listening to each other's tunes, and we were making them sound as good as you possibly could on that humble hardware. The only thing I miss about it is the spirit—not the result.

DotT establishes itself as an interactive cartoon—even the box calls it a "cartoon adventure." And when it comes to making a cartoon in a classical style, the music really sells the action and syncs up with the movements onscreen in a very stylized way. What were some of the challenges of giving the music this much responsibility on a project when early 90s technology could only do so much?

PM: The very biggest challenge was the wide variety of playback systems. I mean, *Day of the Tentacle* had to work on a PCAT, like an 82, 86 chip. I hope I'm remembering these numbers right. When you set up the game, you were still in text mode on a PC. And you had to deal with the fact that some of your audience had a PC that was going to be twice as slow, literally twice as slow [as was recommended]. One of our biggest fans was Steven Spielberg, and every time we'd do a LucasArts game, we'd get a letter from Steven Spielberg saying how much he loved what we did, which was very fun. And Steven had—I hope you don't mind I call him Steven, I never met him—he had a full time guy who kept his game computer. At least this was reputed to be true.

And so, he had the guy who kept his gaming computer system up to scratch, so I'm sure he had the fastest PC and a killer surround sound system, and a great room to play it in. So, we were basically creating games for everybody from Steven Spielberg to play to some college kid who's got a PCAT that they found in a dumpster, and has not even a SoundBlaster but just an AdLib card. As a result, things like cutscenes, they're something that you pretty much take for granted in games these days. It's still not 100 percent, but you essentially take fixed frame rate for granted. You know if the cutscene takes one minute and four seconds on [somebody's PC] at some college dorm somewhere, it's also going to take one minute and four seconds at Steven Spielberg's gaming suite. So timing is something that's more like the movies now than it was then.

But in those days, no matter what the programmers told you, and they did occasionally try to claim otherwise, there was nothing remotely waving at a fixed framerate. So one of the things that the iMUSE system did was to compensate for that by playing longer or shorter versions of the piece depending on how things were progressing in a cutscene. It's weird: iMUSE was famous at that time for being interactive. You do something, and the music does something, and that's sort of exciting. What a lot of people didn't realize was that a lot of the heavy lifting done by iMUSE was to just make it seem like it wasn't interactive at all, to make it seem like a movie playing.

So, if you play the opening cutscene, with the purple tentacle and so on, on one person's machine, it would not look or sound exactly the same as on another's. See, this was before people were playing cutscenes by streaming the video and using a codec. The first LucasArts product to do that, to my knowledge, was *Rebel Assault*. And Vince Lee, who programmed that, he was the first person at Lucas to rather brilliantly see that what you have to do is sync the picture to the sound and not the other way around.

That was a big challenge, to be artistic and write a piece of music that evokes all of the action of evil Dr. Fred doing something or other, and make that work with different kinds of timing. You'd write this little piece that would have little sections that could kind of graze around for a minute before going to the next section. And you would program that up, which was fairly painstaking, and test it on the worst machine in the company, and the best, and see how it worked.

So, would you say the "improvisational" nature of the soundtrack is a safeguard, in a way, for different kinds of technology?

PM: Yeah, pretty much, I think of *Monkey 2*, *Indy 4*, and *DotT* as sort of a trio. And they were very much a trio, because they had constant music, [which was] the expectation in graphic adventures. To achieve the constant music without it having the sense of it being a loop, because we really tried to have forms that weren't obviously loops. And we would look at what other people were doing too. Sierra Online did versions of this as well, where the music had little modules that would play randomly and give you a sense of there being more music than there was. If you start to play a one-minute loop, it's going to be noticeable midway through the second repeat. And that can be pretty mind-numbing.

It can work in some situations, like in a combat situation. But if you're sitting there trying to solve a puzzle... And because *DotT* was a puzzle game, that's a big reason for that perception you have of the music cruising around. You want to give a cartoony effect when there are cartoony moments, but when characters are exploring around, you want it to be kind of ambient. That was basically what we were going for and spending all our effort on, was to keep a variety and have a sense of the music being musical and not just being slavish. But at the same time, if something important happened, the music had to be right there.

Our metaphor was a pit orchestra. I played in a pit orchestra in high school for musicals, and there's a score that everyone's reading in the pit orchestra, but the conductor's always looking over his shoulder to see what's going on on the stage. And, every so often, it'll be like, "Okay, [skip to] measure 32." It's usually not that dramatic, but the tempo—whether or not to take a repeat, all those kind of things—those are judgments that the conductor makes based on what's going on on stage, and show music has little pieces that can play while they're waiting for something to happen, like a curtain call.

The idea of leitmotifs—recurring musical themes attached to characters or settings—weren't new to LucasArts adventure games, but they definitely have the strongest presence in *DotT*. Was the importance of leitmotifs intentional?

PM: The truth is, we did think about that stuff a lot. We were all schooled in that tradition. I say we were schooled in the tradition of Wagner and Looney Tunes, and how Looney Tunes parodied Wagner, Carl Stalling parodied Wagner. And, I think maybe the reason that it's extra noticeable in *Day of the Tentacle* was [because] with Indiana Jones, you're dealing with John Williams themes, which are wonderful, but we were trying to be true to them, so we didn't try to come up with too many new ones. And the way you use leitmotifs is a little different in a movie than in the game, and with something like Monkey [Island], which was much more thematic that way. With Monkey there were a lot of characters and they had themes, but there was this overall vibe of the pirate reggae music that was so dominant that you don't really associate particular melodies with characters as much, with a couple noticeable exceptions like the voodoo lady.

But for *DotT*, it's basically all about the characters. There's a whole team of kids, and each one of them is really interesting, and then of course you have a couple bad guys, and both of them need themes. So we really meant to make that pretty obvious, and that was what was fun about the score. Because the comedy's kind of slapstick, [we had] kind of over-the-top representations of that in the music, so that you always know who's talking. A lot of time we would have little hooks that would play the character's theme if that character was talking, kind of thing.

I interviewed Tim about this game maybe three or four years ago, and he told me that Bernard's theme is taken from a Christian hymn.

PM: [Bernard's theme is] vaguely reminiscent of the Johnny Appleseed music in the Disney cartoon of Johnny Appleseed, and there was, because, the Johnny Appleseed theme goes, [singing] "The Lord's been good to me, and so I thank the Lord, for giving me the things I need, sending the rain and the apple seed, the Lord's been good to me."

There are maybe four or five notes that are the same, yeah.

PM: And mine is, [vocalizes Bernard's theme]. So, it's pretty different. Johnny Appleseed, by the way, he was a Swedenborgian Christian. Emmanuel Swedenborg is a very interesting character, if you ever want to check him out. That sound of joy in the Johnny Appleseed theme, which is much more diatonic and dance-like, or whatever, springtime in the hills sounding. I was certainly going for happiness, but with a more twisted [sound].

While replaying DotT, *I noticed that the music meant to characterize the nerdy Bernard Bernoulli had more than a bit in common with klezmer music found in traditional Jewish culture, and that Bernard himself resembles Woody Allen—a Jewish comedian. (Although Bernard's ethnic background is left undefined by the game, his last name presumably comes from Swiss mathematician/physicist Daniel Bernoulli.) When asked about these influences, McConnell verified that he's a big fan of klezmer music, and that Bernard's physical and musical characteristics were both heavily influenced by Allen.*

With Bernard I do notice a little bit more of—is it called klezmer music?

PM: I think [Bernard's] totally a Woody Allen parody, especially with the glasses. And I think his instrument is generally the clarinet, which Woody Allen plays. And Woody Allen played all that clarinet music in *Sleeper*.

[Allen's] an incredible, incredible player. Really makes you want to kill yourself. So, yeah, I would say there is a little klezmer influence in there. I'm always influenced by 70s crime drama music. I was a huge fan of all those Quinn Martin shows, like *Mannix* and *Cannon* and *Barnaby Jones*, so I was a big Lalo Schifrin fan. A lot of the jazz that you hear is in a Lalo Schifrin vibe with probably a fair amount of *Twilight Zone* influence on *Day of the Tentacle* as well for me. And a little bit of *Hawaii Five-O*. There was a bad guy, a particularly devious bad guy on *Hawaii Five-O*, who had a really great little harpsichord theme, and that may or may not be where I got the idea of Dr. Fred having a harpsichord.

We tried to [give every character their own leitmotif]. They were the MT-32 versions of an instrument. Generally speaking, Hoagie was a rocker, and so we tried to have something that sounded like guitars for him, and I think occasionally tuba. Of course, there were the IRS guys, which is my personal favorite that I did for *DotT*, was the IRS guy theme because it's got this kind of *Get Smart/Pink Panther* vibe to it.

To further its cartoony vibe, *DotT* also employs classical pieces that have come to be known mostly for

their use in animated shorts of the Golden Age of Hollywood.

PM: [We were really] going to the old Looney Tunes tradition of parodying the operatic stuff. "The Rabbit of Seville," and "What's Opera, Doc." So, starting out with Rossini, it seemed like the obvious thing to do, we'd seen so many cartoons that start out with that piece.

There really are two cliches you can put there. One is [vocalizes beginning of "William Tell Overture"], that's the one that we used. And the other is [vocalizes "Morning Mood" by Grieg]. The thing that's fun about it is we did the big giant cliché. We completely ripped off ripping off. Sometimes that's the funniest thing, and it set up perfectly the evil, "you must pay the rent" music for Purple Tentacle. And there's a great example of how that music is actually interactive. That opening scene is so long that where you are in the music when the kids are at a certain point, when that car reaches a certain point on the hill, and you want a gag to happen, you want a stinger, that's completely dependent on the machine that it's playing on.

So, Clint [Bajakian] spent a good amount of time making the piece so that it could gracefully jump ahead or bide its time while the picture caught up. So that all those gags would be assured to happen at the right time. To actually score it like a Carl Stalling score of a cartoon where you're following the motion that minutely took some fancy technology—essentially accounting for the unfanciness of the underlying technology, which wasn't streaming. It was rendering.

I'd like to know what you think of this experience in retrospect, 23 years later, and how do you reflect on your work on this game compared to things you made before and since?

PM: Holy crap, it's 23 years later. Oh, jeez. [laughs] Okay, so you were saying, before and since, I look at it as my introduction to how games get made. And the whole idea of really, really dedicating yourself to the best possible experience that the player's going to have. You know what's great about Disneyland is: Everything about it is fun. Unless it's ridiculously crowded, even waiting in line is fun. They take special care that if there's an opportunity anywhere in that park to make something fun, they'll go out of their way to do that. You'll look down in line, and you'll see some little thing, and you'll go, "Man, that did not have to be there, but that is really cute."

And that's the way we were with those games. Some of that spirit can get lost these days, with games the way they are now. But I think there are people and companies and teams that carry that sort of tradition on, where you basically didn't have to do that, but you did, and because you did, the player has a little smile.

I think that's really what I learned from *DotT* in particular. Because there was a lot of good writing in that game. Just the whole idea of: You don't have to have that sixth useless response in the dialogue tree that still has a great little elbow-nudging punchline, but it's so much better because you do. And I think we did the same thing with the music, even though, given the choice now [between programmed scores and live music performed by human beings], I will always try to do something with human beings.

main creatives behind the game. Perhaps most impressively, Double Fine had access to the original voice recordings from twenty-plus years ago, so *Remastered* presents them in their full, uncompressed glory. They sound like they were recorded yesterday—and if you're used to the fuzzy, low-bitrate voices from the original release, hearing the clarity of the remastered version can be a downright eerie experience.

If you're new to adventure games, the new UI provided by Double Fine (and available in both modern and classic visual interpretations) comes off as a very smart modernization of *DotT*'s original interface. Instead of forcing the player to build a command from a grid of selectable verbs, *DotT*'s updated UI brings up a radial menu of only the possible verbs—eliminating the chaff and making the prospect of experimentation far less daunting. This improved UI works in tandem with *Day of the Tentacle*'s smoothed-over graphics to essentially make the whole package feel like a "new" adventure game—despite its multiple decades on this planet. While the painstakingly detailed sprite graphics seen in the "classic" mode remain gorgeous in all of their low-tech glory, every background and frame of animation has faithfully made the transition to a much higher resolution. Granted, you lose a noticeable amount of the intentionality behind those pixel graphics while using the modernized presentation, but *DotT* veterans can play through this revamped version without necessarily missing the old one. If anything, this stands as a testament to the beauty of *Day of the Tentacle*'s original assets—even three decades later, the sheer amount of art and animation powering each character can stand toe-to-toe with any modern 2D game.

Double Fine went to great lengths to make this version of *Day of the Tentacle* as complete as possible—right down to the inclusion of the original *Maniac Mansion* as the same killer Easter egg found in the original. Hardcore retro sticklers can experience a startlingly accurate simulation of a 1993 video game, while everyone else can play a version of *Tentacle* that feels thoroughly modern. Appealing to new players was wise, seeing as how the original *DotT* did not sell enough copies to automatically ensure the success of a remake. But somehow, within a megacorp consumed by ultra-profitable IP like Marvel and Star Wars, this humble sequel found a fan deep within Disney.

•

The remaster seems like a no-brainer to fans, but it may never have happened if not for the game's champions at Disney, the parent company who now owns all LucasArts properties.

TS: There's a couple people there, like John Vignocchi, who's a fan of those old games, and who was an advocate. So, we had an advocate at Disney to push it through the system. Because, with any big company, they have a lot of bigger fish to fry, and, without someone standing up for your project, it doesn't really work out. So, it was great, both at Disney and at Sony we had people who loved old adventure games, and maybe the thing that it was waiting for was people who were young and played the games and loved them to be old enough to rise to a position with the action to make it happen.

Oliver Franzke, Lead Programmer of *DotT Remastered*, in his GDC 2017 talk: Our process really starts with game archaeology. We essentially identify and sort through lots of files associated with the original project. The team went to Skywalker Ranch in San Francisco to the physical archives to scan some of the original concept art paintings. For me as a programmer, what's much more interesting is the digital game archaeology. The way the archiving process worked in the 90s at LucasArts was that at the end of a project the archiving team would come and take an image of all the developers' computers. So the first step [for us] was to go through this long list of files that were sometimes conflicting, or complimentary, or redundant to come up with a master list that would form the foundation for the remastered version.

TS: It was really really different [than remastering *Grim Fandango*]. *Grim* was such a weird mix of trying to get in there and change things without really reopening the engine and remaking the old stuff, but [still] making things like dynamic lighting work on the characters. It was much more, I feel, a technical magic show. The things that [the team in charge of the remaster] did with that game were kind of magic, and I think *Day of the Tentacle* was a little bit more of a model of what [a remaster] should be like. We had the special editions of [the first two] Monkey Island [games] that came out, and, Oliver, our lead programmer, he had worked on those, so he had worked on that system to crossfade between [the two different visual styles]. We had some idea of what a remastered 2D game should look like because of that. So it was more of a challenge of finding all the old 2D assets and just a lot of painting all those frames. Matt Hansen, the producer on the remaster, can tell you how many frames. A ton of animation.

Oliver Franzke, GDC 2017: Everyone on the remaster team really was a huge fan of these games. We all played them when we were younger, we liked the writing, the humor, the puzzles, and the art style, and we really didn't see any reason to change that. What we did want to change was how easy it was to play these games, and more specifically to make them available on platforms they previously weren't on, like contemporary consoles or mobile devices. While doing that, it was important to us to stay true to the original artistic intent.

We wanted to stay close to the original art style while still using the hardware that we have and its capabilities to create a beautiful modern version of the same game. There are some features that really didn't hold up over the twenty years and we wanted to modernize those delicately so that it conforms to modern standards but the original gameplay is preserved. When the original games shipped in the 90s, they shipped with bugs, and we wanted to take the opportunity to fix as many of these bugs as possible. Lastly, we wanted to do something for hardcore fans. For you, we wanted to add features like developer commentary or the concept art gallery so there's something extra to explore.

DG: I actually did the design for the [remaster's] achievements. They said, "Hey, we need somebody to do this, Dave, will you do it?" So, that was an excuse to play through the whole thing again.

Early in the remastering process, the team considered a big change in the game's visual style before eventually settling on a style much closer to the original: Everything looks the same, only at a higher resolution and with smoother lines.

TS: I did do some early passes on it when it was reimagined, and we didn't like it. It was too rendered, too fancy. I felt what we wanted to do was just clean up the older art, like, take the jaggies off of it, but keep the bold broad strokes of color and not add a lot of fancy rendering to it. So, that's what we did, and I think it showed a lot of restraint on the art team's part that they didn't repaint it all in the way that a modern piece of artwork would be painted. I think they kept it to those hard color barriers, but just smooth edges.

[*Day of the Tentacle Remastered* is] the original engine opened up and with new things added. A lot of the work went into the new interface... a streamlined, modern one that looks a little bit more like *Broken Age*, with a verb dial, like you might expect from some of the later Lucas games, mixed in with the interface [and the] the inventory screen from *Broken Age*. But, you can also switch it back to be exactly like the old one. And these guys went the extra mile to do all combinations of those, so you can actually take the new art, but still have the old interface, so you can have the verbs at the bottom of the screen and the point and click, with the new art. And then, the crazy one is, you can do the old art with the new interface, so there's an 8-bit version of the verb dial. So, the new streamlined interface, but with the pixel art.

Oliver Franzke, GDC 2017: One of our goals was to stay true to the original version, and we actually wanted to run the original gameplay scripts against the original data against the original engine. In other words, we wanted to run the game in a sandbox. As far as *Day of the Tentacle* is concerned, it is still running on a DOS computer in 1993. This design has one major benefit which is that the original design still produces a completely valid frame buffer, which means we can very easily blend between the remastered version and the classic version. This quickly became a fan favorite. People love toggling back and forth between the two versions and comparing them. As a programmer, I find it a little amusing because all we do is blend between two textures and do some translation, but it just shows you that sometimes the simplest feature really can add a lot of value to your game.

Matt Hansen: We wanted to retain [the game's use of the iMUSE system], so part of that process was creating a version of the music that sounds just like it did back in the day when you played it on your SoundBlaster 16. Also, we wanted to do a remastered version that would take some modern technology and make it sound really nice and clean. We were able to, through some different programs and emulation, create a MIDI patch that sounds just like the original SoundBlaster 16 version. We recorded out a bunch of PCM streams that we play dynamically through Fmod, based on the iMUSE events that the game fires off. So it sounds just like it did back in 1993, which is awesome.

And you can seamlessly switch between that old music and the new remastered music. We've now taken high quality samples like you would for modern music composition, and used the old MIDI tracking to play back these new samples. So it sounds like this whole new revoiced version of the music.

TS: At the time [when we were developing the original game], [LucasArts] had an archive room. They had two full-time archivists, even in the floppy days. And there was a room full of drawers with floppy discs [that contained the finished game as well as previous "milestone" drafts], before the end, you would take it down to Wendy [and her team]. They're credited as being the "burning goddesses" in the credits because they burned all the CDs. It was the burning room. They sat there burning CDs all day long. But, in the old days, there was a whole room, and two full-time positions of archiving stuff.

I feel like there was the feeling at LucasArts, because Lucas himself had that archive, the barn, and that's where all the LucasArts stuff is now, is in the barn at the ranch. So, there was that feeling of: Take care of the artifacts of the thing that you're making because you'll want them someday.

•

Touching Up the Past

While the art and animation of Day of the Tentacle *stands as an impressive achievement for 1993, refurbishing the chunky sprite graphics and pixelated backgrounds for the standards of today requires a careful touch. Luckily, both Chan and Ahern assisted the artists at Double Fine by ensuring* DotT's *art successfully made the transition from low to high resolution.*

LA: Basically, they talked to me about converting the characters to high-res versions. I sat down and did some sketches to kind of point them in the right direction for how I would refine the details. If you're taking this pixelated version of the character, what would he look like in high res? How do the small details like the mouth and the tip of the nose and whatever translate? Because sometimes [when] someone's trying to take something to high res, they're guessing. Does the nose split between these two pixels, or does it lean towards one or the other? And sometimes it matters. So, I did some high-res sketches of the three main characters, and then, I also did the new art that's used in marketing stuff. I did the black and white version of that and someone else painted it.

PC: Thankfully, Yujin Kiem, he was hired to help, and his incredible team. Yujin has kept in touch with me, and at the beginning he would email me and share some of the old drawings and the new drawings, and asked what was I thinking. And so, we went back and forth, and I shared my thoughts. "This is the reason why I did this and that," and Yujin got it. He was brilliant. Yujin studied my stuff enough to see where I was going with it, and he got into the spirit of things, and I think he passed that down to his team. I think those guys did an amazing job of cleaning up and doing everything that I wish I could have done twenty years ago.

Oliver Franzke, GDC 2017: Despite what some people on the internet might claim, the remastered art is not created though some automatic process—an upscaling filter or something. People on our team will get very angry if you ask them that. Every single image has been hand-crafted by an artist. [...] There were nearly 8,000 animation sprites that had to be repainted. We knew from the beginning we wouldn't be able to handle this internally. Our art department was pretty small, and they were all busy remastering the environments. We sent [the original files] off to the outsourcing company, they then painted over those, and once they were happy, they sent it back to us and we ran an automatic export process to extract all the remastered sprites.

LA: It's funny, because I actually stumbled across a play-through video interview with Tim the other day, and, they had the interview in the main screen, and then a window in the corner showing the game that they were playing through, and they were playing through the high-res version, and, like, when I've looked at the high-res version myself, I kind of go, "Yeah, that's pretty good, but I liked the original better," because there's a certain amount of just blending and averaging. It feels like this has been averaged on some level, and it may not be exactly the way I would have done it. But then I saw it in that little inset, and I realized, oh, it looks fantastic there. If I get too close to it and nitpick the details, I'm like, "Ah, I wouldn't have done it that way," but when I can step back from worrying about that stuff, I thought it looked fantastic. So I'm sure anybody but the person who designed it will love it.

PC: What I also appreciate is [that] the [fans of the original game] who are playing it have this nostalgic feeling for it, and the last thing I wanted to do was clean it up so much that it's unrecognizable. I didn't want to do that. I didn't want to change it. I just wanted it to be cleaned up a little bit here and there, but I wanted to keep that old nostalgic feeling because that's what they grew up with, and that's what the fans want. It's like the old Star Wars. Just leave the old Star Wars alone. So that was the goal: Try to be true to it as much as you can so then the fans could hopefully still appreciate it.

The remasters were a hit with old and new fans alike. According to Franzke in his 2017 GDC talk, combined sales of the remastered editions of Tentacle *and* Grim Fandango *exceeded five million units, making both remasters more successful than the originals.*

DAY OF THE TENTACLE

IT TOOK ON THE WORLD

DAY OF THE TENTACLE never had the widest reach. Both *DotT* and its predecessor made their respective waves specifically within the very narrow category of point-and-click adventure games. (A genre designation referring to an innovation old enough to have a mid-life crisis.) And because of this, it's often overlooked. The mention of *Day of the Tentacle* won't spark the same immediate recognition as, say, *Super Mario Bros.* or *Sonic the Hedgehog*, and in telling people about this project, my description started as "you know, the sequel to *Maniac Mansion*," then moved to "well, it's kind of like *Monkey Island*," and eventually landed on "trust me, it's very cool."

For decades, *DotT* was only available on a single platform, and for many years most people had to resort to piracy to play it. Despite the quality of the experience, it's rare to find *Day of the Tentacle* on one of those ubiquitous "best games of all time" lists. You may see *The Secret of Monkey Island* or even *Maniac Mansion* included for how much they refined the genre, but *DotT* often gets viewed as just part of the consistently beloved library of LucasArts adventures.

Yet *Day of the Tentacle* stands out as an adventure game made by an amazing team who put the lessons learned from *Monkey Island* 1 and *2* into practice while pushing against the limits of what mere diskettes could hold. Released on the cusp of the multimedia era, *Day of the Tentacle* shines as an early example of the direction games would be going before many of them were dragged kicking and screaming into the world of CD-ROM. The squat characters from the Indiana Jones and Monkey Island games have been replaced by large, expressive ones with many animations. Especially given its release date, *Day of the Tentacle* does an elegant job of simulating another medium—in this case, a Saturday morning cartoon—while remaining incredibly interactive.

Day of the Tentacle may have influenced the future of art direction at LucasArts (simply by having such a thing as art direction), but it's unfortunate that the quality of its design stands alone in this era. Tim Schafer and Dave Grossman absorbed the rules of adventure game design by working directly under Ron Gilbert, and with this knowledge, the two directors went back to one of LucasArts' earliest hits to see how they could improve on it. The result is one of the developer's last games in which an attempt to be "cinematic" does not get in the way of the game's design. No other LucasArts adventure would have you controlling three characters independently, let alone across three different time periods.

The company's following games all chose very different ways to articulate the concept of "adventure game" instead of building off of the game design master class that is *Day of the Tentacle*. The very rushed *Sam & Max Hit the Road* amounted to a sprawling, messy quest that culminates in a fairly uninspired scavenger hunt. The famously troubled *The Dig* carries a fantastic atmosphere but offers puzzles that feel like *Myst* rejects. And Schafer's next project, *Full Throttle*, aspires to be cinematic above any other trait, leaving the player with an experience far less interactive than previous LucasArts adventures. 1996's *The Curse of Monkey Island* would act as a fine return to form before the era of polygonal games presented some new problems for adventure games—one that would require an entirely different book to cover.

All of these games have value, but *Day of the Tentacle* had the advantage of being made before LucasArts felt a need to "reinvent" the adventure game, and instead simply made the very best adventure game they could. Everyone at LucasArts still operated under Lucas's directive of, "Stay small, be the best, and don't lose any money."

Thankfully for Schafer and Grossman, *Day of the Tentacle* didn't lose money, and immediately after its development, the two found themselves pitching more games to the suits at LucasArts. Grossman would unfortunately end up working on one of several unreleased versions of *The Dig*, while Schafer would produce *Full Throttle*, LucasArts's most successful game by far. After directing 1998's *Grim Fandango*, Tim went on to found the developer Double Fine—which has now been going strong for over twenty years—and he remains an incredibly accomplished (not to mention very affable) public figure in the world of video games.

Grossman might not be as much of a public game industry figure as Schafer, but he went on to make quality adventure games under his old boss Ron Gilbert at Humongous Entertainment, and helped lead Telltale's revival of the Sam & Max series through the mid to late 00s. The reserved yin to Schafer's boisterous yang, Grossman maintained a poem of the week blog/mailing list for close to twenty years, and even self-published a collection titled *Ode to the Stuff in the Sink: A Book of Guy Poetry* in 2002. He currently holds the role of CCO at Earplay, which creates interactive audio dramas. And in a move that will shock no one, Grossman returned to his adventure game roots working next to Ron Gilbert with a role as designer and writer on the unexpected 2022 sequel, *Return to Monkey Island*.

Recent years have seen *DotT*'s great design and humor in other games worked on by its key creative staff. The re-releases of Telltale's *Sam & Max* series serve as a nice reminder that Dave Grossman never lost his knack for creating adventure games, as does the stellar *Return to Monkey Island*, which contains some of the best puzzle design the series has ever seen. And speaking of long-awaited sequels, Tim Schafer's *Psychonauts 2* pairs his always-snappy writing with some great gameplay—the latter of which couldn't always be found in the 2005 original. Some 30 years after the release of their first game as project leads, it's heartening to know that both creators are still doing great work, and with the same qualities found in their 1993 debut.

By the time of *DotT*'s release, Peter McConnell's soundtracks had already become an expected feature of any LucasArts game, and the 90s saw him create an incredible amount of memorable music for the developer until the end of their adventure game era. But even more than twenty years removed from his former stomping grounds, McConnell has never strayed too far from his old friends. The composer has consistently worked for Tim Schafer's Double Fine Productions since their first project, *Psychonauts*, up through their most recent release, *Psychonauts 2*. And McConnel returned to compose for yet another long-awaited sequel in 2022: *Return to Monkey Island*. Even all these decades later, the LucasArts adventure game experience isn't complete without his contributions.

The 2016 release of *Day of the Tentacle Remastered* released to critical praise and modest success, but for some people—*especially* me—this remake justified all the praise I'd been heaping on the game since I first played it twenty years ago. Not only did it give people a new way to play this classic, it also gave me the opportunity to talk to just about everyone involved in its creation. I set out to craft a definitive history of *Day of the Tentacle* that would offer proof of its greatness, so hopefully by this point you're fully convinced. If not, please return to page one and start over from the beginning. Unlike in worlds with power-hungry tentacles, that's the only kind of time travel our current reality allows.

The original 2016 publishing of my *Day of the Tentacle* oral history represented a big turning point in my life. As someone who won the employment lottery and obtained one of the ever-diminishing jobs in games media, I'd also been fortunate enough to put together a project I'd been dreaming of for a decade. But this fulfilling work also existed alongside my main duty: writing much smaller pieces that would inevitably be consumed and forgotten by the daily cycle of content churn. Assembling this dream project on top of my full-time gig (along with other side hustles) pushed me to my limit, and caused me to work a seriously unhealthy number of hours. I'd been used to seeing the slate wiped clean after lots of needless overworking, but going back to treading water in the world of online media a day after completing this just broke my heart. In this internet ecosystem, my exploration of *DotT* was destined to be pushed off the front page and out of readers' minds just as quickly as a written preview for some annualized sequel.

A year after writing the original version of this oral history, I left the press behind to focus on podcasting full-time, which has given me more opportunities to talk to my heroes—and also gave me and my editors at Boss Fight Books the chance to improve upon a large chunk of writing initially composed by a much more tired and miserable version of myself.

As of this writing, USgamer, the website that once featured the first version of this oral history, recently took the same path as most defunct video game websites. Its content has been scrubbed from the face of the internet, and what little remains exists in the form of whatever the Internet Archive could grab before doomsday. I started the project thanks to the slightly selfish urge to preserve my favorite piece of writing, and thanks to Boss Fight Books, it can now live on in a form less fly-by-night than online media. For that, I'm incredibly grateful—and hey, the next time Wikipedia wants to cite me, they can point to something other than a dead link. If that's not proof that I exist, I don't know what is.

A CHOOSE-YOUR-OWN-AFTERWORD BY TIM SCHAFER

1. If you skipped here before reading this book, please go to paragraph 253a. If you read the whole book and are now reading this, please go to paragraph 638b.

5k. Did I mention that one of the dead whales had an idea that would have cured all known disease? The End.

10x. The ship's cargo hold, being full of Magnesium-based fireworks, burns even in the water, killing a nearby family of blue whales. Go to 275r.

12c. I think that phone number had too many digits. Go to 987k.

19d. I'm not putting my lips on that. You are dead.

23a. If you're reading this paragraph, then you have cheated! Nothing points to this. Congratulations.

You've hacked the book. You must be so proud of yourself, undoing the work of beleaguered game designers yet again. Or can't you follow simple instructions? Or are you just a rebel? I have to admit, I do admire your *je ne sais quoi*, your *joie de vivre*, your IDGAF. But still, the rules are clear on this point. You cheated, and must go back to the very first page of the book and start all over again.

28u. Those two things won't work together... yet. The game has crashed.

34f. Now that his hair's short, it begs the question—is the bird dead? Go to 987k.

34g. Why did I add letters to these paragraph numbers? Oh well, too late to get rid of them now. Better add this one so it looks like I did it on purpose.

34h. One more, just to be safe.

35g. Unfortunately, the fuse runs out before you cut the final wire and the bomb explodes. Go to 10x.

130p. YOU'RE overrated. Please close this book and give it to someone with better taste. Shouldn't be hard to find! (What? I don't get to have feelings? Okay, I'll give you one more chance. Go back and play *Day of the Tentacle* again and answer the previous question one more time. Hope you don't get stuck in an infinite loop!)

189v. It's kind of gross that you even thought about making this choice. You're lucky that I'm just a book and can't call the cops. Please put this book down and consider turning yourself in to the police, a monastery, or a nunnery. Whichever you think would be funnier.

201f. Unfortunately, every year the lemur-folk ceremoniously devour their king and elect a new one. Go to 487j.

253a. Ah, I was afraid of this. The magnetism of my name has drawn you past the nutritious meal of this fine book, straight to the sweet, sweet dessert. I was afraid of readers like you, but if I am being truthful, then I must admit to myself that I... depend on readers like you. But first, some business I must clear up: Dave Grossman does not, in fact, have a robotic arm as claimed in chapter 3. This is a common misconception because of Dave's undefeated string of victories in office arm wrestling competitions, and also the constant buzzing, clicking, and whirring sounds that Dave emits while moving his arm. Those sounds are made by a tiny lyrebird that lives in Dave's luxurious hair. Just a regular old arm, folks! Sorry. Also, there is no proof that Larry Ahern's "missing weekend" was caused by an alien abduction, and it was definitely not "confirmed by the FBI, NSA, and a bunch of agencies you've never even heard of," like Larry said. Now please go to 34f.

269b. That idea is so brilliant, the game designers didn't even think of it. That means those losers are fired and you get to take over their jobs! This is your game now. You can never leave until you manage to trick someone else into reading this.

275r. The explosion tosses your body clear to a deserted island populated only by intelligent lemurs, who make you their king! Go to 201f.

280l. Aw, you're so sweet. Don't tell the others, but you're my favorite person who's read this afterword. Nobody else has gotten this far! At least not in this copy of the book. If you got this far then please take a pen and cross out the previous part about nobody getting this far. That way it will always be true. In the world of video games, this is what's known as "a patch." Thank you for playing! And reading! Now close the book and go to sleep!

429h. Wow, I hope your rent is really cheap where you live, which must be *under a rock*! Anyway, I hope reading this book makes you want to play *Day of the Tentacle*. Please put this book down, go play *DotT*, then come back and answer the previous question again. We'll be here, waiting. I promise.

487j. Luckily, before you die, you write a memoir that, when found years later, becomes a posthumous best-seller, making your estranged, ungrateful children (who never searched for you) happy for as long as it takes them to blow the money on deadly vices. Go to 5k.

555n. If you go here, go back and check your math.

638b. I admire your discipline, dear reader. You must be the type of person who plays entire adventure games without looking at the hint book once! Do you have any idea how much harm you've caused to hint book sales? How many 1-800-STAR WARS phone operators you've put out of work? Think about their children. But don't call them. That would be creepy. Please go to 12c.

705s. Make a Charisma saving throw. If you succeed, look in the mirror, gently pretend to punch yourself in the chin, and wink at yourself. You earned it. If you failed, welcome to the club, buddy. Either way, game over.

987k. I loved working on *Day of the Tentacle*. As the years go by, I feel more and more proud that I got to be part of it. Dave Grossman was such a fun, intelligent, and easy-going creative partner. Larry and Peter were such talented artists. Peter, Clint, and Michael's music was perfect. The world created by Ron and Gary was so rich for exploration. Everybody at LucasArts back then just wanted to add more fun to the game. "How can we make this better?" There was so much enthusiasm, it was like we were a bunch of teenagers making a float for the homecoming parade. At least, that's what I imagine high school sports events were like. I was too busy in the computer club. But it was definitely collaborative, the team was imaginative, the technology was ready, the river was polluted, and the tentacles were thirsty! Everything came together to make an incredibly special creative experience. If you played *Day of the Tentacle* and loved it, please go to 280l. If you played *Day of the Tentacle* and think it's overrated, please go to 130p. If you haven't played *Day of the Tentacle*, go to 429h.

2112b. Was a great side of a great album by Rush. Some would say that side A was better, being the epic narrative side. But side B has "A Passage to Bangkok," which really holds up to this day as a single, apart from its questionable "ethnic instrumentation." I didn't even realize that it was about drugs at the time. How innocent was I?

3005t. "I guess you were my son the whole time," the Hawklass says with a screech. She releases her talons to set you free. Unfortunately, you were lying about being her son and you cannot fly after all. You are dead.

NOTES

Much of the content of this book comes from developer interviews I conducted for an oral history first published by USgamer.net in 2016 and now archived at VG247 (http://bit.ly/3wsUdsn). Many of the quotes from those interviews appear in this book for the first time. A bit more comes from my review of *Day of the Tentacle Remastered*, also first published by USgamer.net in 2016 (http://bit.ly/3WygnE9), as well as my 2015 interview retrospective with Ron Gilbert, first published by USgamer.net in 2015 (http://bit.ly/3R3cpT7). Quotes in the book come from my interviews unless otherwise mentioned. Quotes have been lightly edited for clarity and concision.

Oliver Franzke's 2017 GDC talk, "Remastering Day of the Tentacle and Grim Fandango," was published to YouTube on October 16, 2017: https://bit.ly/3iZsg8F

Ron Gilbert's 2011 GDC talk, "Classic Game Postmortem: Maniac Mansion," was published to YouTube on March 30, 2017: https://bit.ly/3XEXEbr

Dave Grossman and Tim Schafer appeared on Episode 19 of Brett Douville and Tim Longo's podcast, DGC: Dev Game Club, on July 13, 2016. http://bit.ly/3kEJs3E

Tim Schafer was interviewed in 2012 by John Walker for Rock, Paper, Shotgun in an article titled "Interview: Tim Schafer On Adventures," published on February 28, 2012: http://bit.ly/3XZVKCe

Day of the Tentacle Remastered comes with a developer's commentary track, which is quoted occasionally in the book.

Tim Schafer was interviewed in 2006 by Ryan Scott for Computer Gaming World Issue 265 in the article, "The CGW Interview: Tim Schafer: Gaming's Rogue Comedian Talks Timing," which appears on pages 44-45.

Dave Grossman was interviewed in 2014 by Retro Gamer Team for Retro Gamer in an article titled "The Making of Day of the Tentacle," published on December 25, 2014: http://bit.ly/3kz0WOK

I interviewed Tim Schafer and Dave Grossman for episode 56 of the podcast, *Retronauts*, which was then hosted by 1UP. com: http://bit.ly/3R8t4on

ACKNOWLEDGEMENTS

Thanks to Liz Lerner for the invaluable interview transcriptions.

Thanks to Boss Fight Books for their generous deadline extension policy. The creation of this book encompassed some pretty strange and difficult years on this planet, but here we are. Special thanks to Gabe Durham, Michael P. Williams, Mike Sholars, David L. Craddock, Meghan Burklund, Nick Sweeney, and Joe M. Owens, who helped elevate this work from mere website articles to the book you're currently holding.

Thanks to all of the interview subjects whose contributions were invaluable to this book: Tim Schafer, Dave Grossman, Peter Chan, Larry Ahern, and Peter McConnell. Oh, and thanks for making *Day of the Tentacle*.

Extra thanks to Larry Ahern and Tim Schafer for contributing to this project seven years after their initial interviews. It's the added touch that truly proves I didn't make everything up.

Thanks to my mom, who will enjoy seeing this at the end of the book. And for not minding how much time I spent on the computer.

Thanks to Mrs. Fisher, my second grade teacher, who gave me a copy of *Ozma of Oz* with the inscription, "Bobby, Maybe you'll write a book, one day!" It seemed oddly prophetic. (Note: 34 years later, and I still haven't read *Ozma of Oz*. Not my thing.)

Thanks to Jon Hicks and Kat Bailey at USgamer for confirming the rights to my original oral history.

SPECIAL THANKS

For making our sixth season of books possible, Boss Fight Books would like to thank A Reynolds, Aaron Murray, Alex Baughn, Alex Cox, Alex Wreschnig, Andreia "shana" Gaita, Andrew Evans, Andrew L, Andrew Mildahl, bluebomber1313@gmail.com, Brent M. Diskin, Brian Fishman, Brice Gilbert, Casey Lawler, Cathy Durham, cecilnick, César Augusto Rivera P., Chris Ayers, Chris Hertling, Christian Rohde, Colbin Erdahl, Collin Banko, Conor Lastowka, Corey Losey, Craig Snyder, Dave T, David Louis, Donald Hopkins, Dr Derek Bulner, Drew Petersen, Dylan Joseph Lee Catania, Elliesberlinkey, Erik Malinowski, Felicity Chevalier, Forrest Greenwood, Graham Faught, Graham Guletz, Greg Cobb, Greg Mattson, In memory of Nicole, J. Kyle Pittman, Jake W Landis, jamiza, Jared Cherup, Jason Boyer, Jay and Problems, JediGameFreak, Jeff Methot, Jeff Peterson, Joe Alonzo - RadJunk, Joel W, Jonathan Blue, Jose Olivenca, Joseph 'UnparalleledDev' Silberstein, Juan Morales-Rocha, Justin K Cole, Justin

Tsang, Kelly Brown, Lasse Bruun Hansen, Leigh Chang, Liz Walsh, Lost In Cult, Lou Sementa, Lucy Lin, Mario Diaz de la Rosa, Mark Kuchler, Mark Sztainbok, Matt Leung, Matthew Ratzloff, Max Weltz, Michael B Jones, Michael Strickland, Michael Tashbook, Mike Janes, Mitchel Labonté, Nathan Asper, Nevan Hartle, Nicholas Payne, Nick Chester, Nick Eliopulos, Nick Folkman, Nicole Amato, Patrick Trevathan, Paul DerHagopian, Quest4Best Wayne III, realslimjd, RegularDude, Rocco Buffalino, Ross Stinemetz, Russell Wiley, Ryan Adams, Ryan Shelby, S. O'Rourke Scott Mendenko, Sean Flannigan, Sean M. Morrow, Stephen Trinh, Topher Davis, and Wes Young.

ALSO FROM BOSS FIGHT BOOKS

1. *EarthBound* by Ken Baumann
2. *Chrono Trigger* by Michael P. Williams
3. *ZZT* by Anna Anthropy
4. *Galaga* by Michael Kimball
5. *Jagged Alliance 2* by Darius Kazemi
6. *Super Mario Bros. 2* by Jon Irwin
7. *Bible Adventures* by Gabe Durham
8. *Baldur's Gate II* by Matt Bell
9. *Metal Gear Solid* by Ashly & Anthony Burch
10. *Shadow of the Colossus* by Nick Suttner
11. *Spelunky* by Derek Yu
12. *World of Warcraft* by Daniel Lisi
13. *Super Mario Bros. 3* by Alyse Knorr
14. *Mega Man 3* by Salvatore Pane
15. *Soft & Cuddly* by Jarett Kobek
16. *Kingdom Hearts II* by Alexa Ray Corriea
17. *Katamari Damacy* by L. E. Hall
18. *Final Fantasy V* by Chris Kohler